Eric,

Live your dreams!

Tye Mane

5/18/07

# Forget Patience,
## Let's Sell Something

**!**

Essential Skills for Winning

More Clients Now!

Tye Maner

Friesens Corporation

*Forget Patience, Let's Sell Something!*

Copyright ©2005 by Tye Maner & Associates, Inc. a Florida Corporation.

First Edition 2005.

Library of Congress Control Number Pending

ISBN Number 978-0-9744880-0-3

Published in Tampa, Florida by Tye Maner & Associates, Inc.

Printed and bound in Canada by Friesens Corporation.

Creative design and illustrations by:
JFD Advertising and Public Relations
600 S. Magnolia Ave., Suite 350
Tampa, FL 33606
813.223.4545
www.jfdadvertising.com

# Acknowledgements

I would like to extend heartfelt love and gratitude to my family for their support, understanding and encouragement as I labored to complete this project. Mom, I also have to thank you for never allowing me to use the word "can't" unless I first removed the "t" from "can't."

Lastly, I have to thank the men from my accountability group: Jim, Del and Duane, who helped me stay the course.

# Table of Contents

"Things come to those who wait, but only the things left by those who hustle."

– *Abraham Lincoln*

# Introduction

## Starving to Death in the Middle of the Feast

I have heard the story of a research study that involved the Northern Pike fish. The pike fish is a very aggressive fish which has a mouth full of teeth. The pike is a proficient hunter. According to the study, a pike was placed in an aquarium with a large supply of it's natural food source: minnows. For two days the pike enjoyed dining on the minnows at will. He devoured the minnows whenever he felt the urge. He ate to his heart's content. On the third day, a glass divider was placed between the pike and the minnows. The pike would hit his snout against the glass every time he attempted to pursue a minnow. This exercise went on for two days. This had to be frustrating for him to be so close, yet so far. On the fifth day, the glass divider was removed. The pike had not eaten for two days. He was unbelievably hungry at this point. An abundance of food was now available. Now those hunger pangs could finally be appeased.

Logically, we would expect him to pursue the minnows and provide sustenance to his body. Unfortunately, the pike fish refused to pursue the minnows. The only way this pike would eat was if a blind minnow swam into his mouth. This poor fish ultimately starved to death with food swimming all around him. All he had to do was reach out and grab it. The pike starved to death in the midst of a feast.

At first glance, it would be easy to say, "What a dumb fish!" Yet I have observed thousands of salespeople imitate that dumb fish. I have even imitated that "dumb fish" on a few occasions.

Let's compare the pike phenomenon to salespersons. Let's say for a moment the salesperson is you. You are in a booming economy and everything is going your way. Or you are on an unbelievable winning streak. Everything you touch turns to gold. All of a sudden the economy turns or you lose three or four sales that you were confident you would win. Like the pike, you become frustrated at the turn of events. You are tired of the rejection. You become fearful of being denied again. So you do nothing. You drive through your territory but you don't stop at any of the buildings which are laden with companies which may have a need for what you provide. You stop doing the things that once brought you success even though you are surrounded by opportunity.

You may be reading this book and are currently performing well in the sales profession. Congratulations on your success. However, you must continue your professional development in order to stay on top. This book will help to elevate your performance whether you are at the top of your game or struggling.

*Forget Patience, Let's Sell Something!* is more than just a self-help book. The purpose of this book is also to be a professional reference guide that you revisit on a regular basis. It is my desire and belief that you will walk away with innovative ideas, tremendous techniques, and sustainable skills that will elevate you to the next level in your quest to be the best.

CHAPTER ONE

# Your Attitude and the Company You Keep

Let me start by saying that volumes have been written and spoken relative to the importance of a positive attitude. It is my sincere belief that the right attitude is truly the major differentiator between those who experience lives of happiness, fullness and consistent long term success, as opposed to those who fall by the wayside on the highway of life, never reaching their full potential or accomplishing the goals they set out to achieve. The statement was once made, "Whether you think you can or think you can't, either way you are right."

The proper attitude causes us to persevere while others quit. It forces us to move forward in spite of obstacles and fears, both large and small. It makes us focus on the things that really matter. A proper attitude helps us keep life's ups and downs in the proper perspective. Life does not care about the attitude we choose, for our life is only a mirror that reflects who we really are by our actions, more so than our words. The choices you make and the company you keep heavily impact your attitude.

*Get fired up about life and its opportunities, or you'll be hosed down by life and its obstacles.*

## A Story of Two Salespersons

Let me tell you the story of Mark and Madeleine. When I began my career in sales, a more experienced salesperson in my office by the name of Mark mentored me. Mark was a very likeable guy. He was happy-go-lucky, and had a great sense of humor. He had one of the best territories in the office. However, Mark's performance and sales volume were mediocre at best. He complained about how bad the economy was. He was frustrated that no one was interested in our products. He felt our price was too high, therefore we weren't competitive in the marketplace.

Mark normally left the office around 9:30 a.m. to get to his territory. His territory was 45 minutes to an hour away from the office. Therefore, he usually made his first sales call around 10:30 a.m. He made a few cold calls and took off for lunch around 11:00 a.m. Mark would then go to one of the local restaurants and have a leisurely meal. After his meal, he would then find himself at one of the local video game arcades where he would unwind before continuing with the drudgery of cold calling on people who really didn't want to see him anyway.

He would always promise himself that he would only play video games for an hour, and then get back to work. The hour turned into an hour and a half, which turned into two hours. There were many times when Mark would meet up with another salesperson from the office and they would goof off together. Misery and mediocrity enjoy the company of others. Instead of being the beacon in the office that spurred others to increase their level of performance, Mark attempted to sabotage those around him to underperform. It was easier to mask his nonperformance if everyone else was underachieving also. Needless to say, Mark's activities (or lack of activity) during the day were the reasons for his lackluster performance.

After spending many dollars and hours being unproductive, Mark would make a few more sales calls, and try to leave his territory around 3:45 so that he could beat rush hour traffic and make it back to the office by 5:00 p.m.

Mark's day wasn't over just yet. He had to take another 45 minutes to an hour to falsify his call reports because of the calls he didn't make. *In most cases, people work harder at trying to get out of work.*

It was always interesting to watch Mark the last week of the month. He would walk into the office totally focused. He had that "deer in the headlights" look in his eyes; afraid that he wouldn't make enough money to cover his draw, or make a commission check. What happened to the funny guy who kept us laughing, the one who was never in a hurry? This was the one week during the month that Mark would leave the office early and return late from his territory. If he only he had that attitude and sense of urgency the first week of a month, how different the results would have been. "I just need to cover my draw," was a common reply.

Some who read this may ask the questions, "What's the big deal? Who did he really affect other than himself?" Actually, Mark impacted several people. Mark was cheating everyone. He cheated himself and his family out of a better quality of life. He cheated customers and prospective customers out of possible solutions that could help improve the performance of their staff, help their company reduce operating cost, and provide them with an improved image in the eyes of their customers. He cheated our company out of increased profits, and greater market share. During times of economic downturn, Mark's actions could cause many people to lose their jobs. The list of people impacted are:
- Administrative and support staff
- Manufacturing staff
- Warehouse staff
- Transportation staff
- Service/repair staff

*"Nothing happens until somebody sells something."*

Mark impacted impressionable new salespersons to underperform. Well, what was the outcome? Mark left the company, never achieving the true greatness that was in him. He starved to death in the midst of a feast.

Mark is not an exception. It is at this point in most careers when individuals who are failing decide to make a change. They change territories, jobs, careers, companies, cities, etc. They believe the problem lies with everything and everybody but themselves. They say to themselves and others, "If only I had this territory, worked for this company, lived in this city, things would be better." Instead of changing his surroundings, he just needed to change his attitude.

Isn't it interesting how the grass usually looks greener on the other side of the fence? In many cases, once we get over to the other side where the grass looked greener, we find that it is greener because there is a lot more manure in the field.

**Figure 1. The grass always looks greener in the other pasture.**

Even if the grass truly is greener, it still must be cut. As a matter of fact, greener grass requires far more work to maintain. There is no easy way to long-term success. Why not apply that care to the territory or position you already possess and are familiar with rather than start anew somewhere else? The learning curve is far less and the return on your effort far quicker. We must eventually learn the lesson that it normally takes more effort to get greater results.

We often try to address the symptoms rather than the root of our problems.

The interesting thing about life is that it will return to you only what you put into it. No more, no less. It has been said that it is impossible to harvest corn if you planted tomatoes. I heard Zig Ziglar make the following statement:

*"If you are easy on yourself, life will be hard on you. If you are hard on yourself, life will be easier on you, and more enriching."*

If you are willing to pay the price and sacrifice, you will be amazed how much more you can accomplish by having the right attitude.

Madeleine, on the other hand was very diligent in her work. She was always positive, and looked for the positive in all situations. She never got involved in the "pity parties" or "parking lot conferences" the rest of the salespersons engaged in. You know, the meetings where the group gets together and talks about how unfair the manager is; about how the company should have a better compensation plan, then we could really make some money; about how if it wasn't raining so much then maybe we could make more calls. Although cordial, Madeleine never wasted much time "chewing the fat." She had goals, and it was clear to everyone that she was intent on accomplishing every one of them.

She was conscientious enough to leave the office in time to arrive in her territory by 8:00 a.m. As a result, she was making her first sales call by 9:00 a.m. Most days she took less than an hour for lunch.

Madeleine also made a habit of making one sales call after 5:00 p.m. This proved to be a very successful practice because in many instances she would find the decision maker in the office alone. The decision makers were really impressed that a salesperson was actually working after 5:00. Another aspect of Madeleine making the calls after 5:00 was the fact that she caught the decision maker with his or her guard down as they were unwinding from the day. Also, in most cases, the phone was no longer ringing, which meant she had their undivided attention.

Madeleine would be the first to confess that she was not the most eloquent speaker, nor did she give the best presentations. "I'm not a race horse, just a plow horse," insisted Madeleine. "I just keep plodding along."

I would immediately think of the tortoise and the hare story every time she would make that comment. Remember the story of the rabbit and the tortoise were in a race? The quick hare took off leaving the slow tortoise in the dust by a mile. The hare was so confident of his victory that he took frequent breaks to goof off, and even took a nap, thinking to himself that he had plenty of time in the race. The tortoise was very slow but beat the rabbit by being methodical, steady, and consistent. Madeleine made the most of every day, and every day gave her a bountiful return. How bountiful? Madeleine did three times the sales volume and made three times the commission that Mark did in the same territory. She got back in abundance what she planted.

It got to the point where it was embarrassing to get beaten by her every month for Salesperson of the Month. She won that honor five consecutive months. Madeleine raised the level of performance in the office by her example. It became obvious to the rest of the sales team that we were going to have to beat her at her own game. We planned to fight fire with fire.

Those of us with a competitive nature refused to stand by and be beaten every month. We began coming to the office earlier, getting to our territory earlier, taking shorter lunches, and making a sales call after 5:00 p.m. This was war, and war called for extreme measures.

Ultimately, no one person dominated as the top salesperson. The funny thing is we all started making so much money because of our newfound commitment to success that it didn't matter as much if we didn't win Salesperson of the Month. A large commission check was a worthy consolation prize.

The energy in our office soared. We became one of the top districts in our region, and in the country. Within a short period of time, everyone was promoted out of that office and into various management positions.

The first change in the non-performers was their attitude. The attitude adjustment provoked a change in action. The change in action caused a change in altitude.

## Attitude + Action = Altitude

It is a false belief that if you just have a positive attitude, you will go far in life. I have seen salespersons who are cheerful, outgoing, and possess a great attitude who never accomplish much. In countless interviews with prospective salespersons, they stated that their enjoyment in meeting people would lend itself to a successful sales career. The Greeters at Wal-Mart enjoy meeting people also, however, I may not hire them for my sales force.

Key Learning:
***You become like the people with whom you associate.***

Can one person make a difference? Absolutely! Are you making a difference?

## The Reasons for Madeleine's Success

Let's review the reasons behind Madeleine's Success;
1. Positive attitude
2. A strong work ethic
3. Focused on her goals
4. Excellent time management
5. Solid sales skills

The question comes to mind, why do we fail to achieve? In most instances, it is because of fear: fear of failure, even fear of success. Let's discuss these two fears in greater detail.

## Fear of Failure

Fear is a natural human emotion that affects each of us at some point or another in our lives. In many cases, fear can actually save our lives by initiating the "Fight or Flight" instinct. Whether we flee or fight, fear evokes action of some kind. The unhealthy type of fear is the kind that paralyzes us from taking action. For example, if I know that I am usually nervous or fearful when it comes to giving presentations, I should use the element of fear to spur me to put in extra time practicing and rehearsing to ensure that the presentation goes well. The action taken will cause me to perform better. Unfortunately, many of us would allow fear to prevent us from giving presentations at all. If you are fearful about investing, take the action necessary to learn more about investing by reading on the subject, hiring a financial advisor, or becoming a part of an investment group or club. Invest in low risk vehicles instead of high risk vehicles, but take action. It is only natural to desire to avoid pain. Failing at anything is painful. It is one thing to fail at something when you are the only one aware of your failure. Unfortunately, that is not normally the case. I believe society has made us feel that mistakes are bad. The most successful people I know personally and have read about are the individuals who accepted their failures as opportunities to learn. What they learn gives them an opportunity to do that thing they have failed at in a different and better way.

## Fear of Success

I have worked with many salespersons who felt that success always seemed to be just out of their grasp. In reality, they were afraid of success. They were fearful of crossing the threshold into the realm of success. This type of salesperson is concerned that if they excel, then they are expected to perform at the higher level on a consistent basis. Their success brings with it added pressure to continue to exceed their goals, or to be a leader. It may even mean the possibilities of a promotion, which causes additional exposure. Therefore, it is safer to stay below the surface of excellence. There is a quote from the Bible that states, "To whom much is given, much is required."

CHAPTER TWO

# What is Selling?

Selling is a profession made up of three primary components. Selling is an art, a science, and a career.

## Selling as an Art

It is an art because it allows for personal creativity. As I travel around the country working with thousands of salespeople, I find it invigorating and exciting to see the different ideas that they generate. What is more important than the idea itself is the implementation of the idea. The following are stories of individuals who took action.

There was one salesperson in North Carolina who attempted to contact the CEO of a company. After doing some research, he found out that the CEO was an avid runner. He also found out the shoe size of the executive. He then went out and bought some very nice running shoes and sent one shoe to the executive. When the executive received the one shoe, he was so excited he ran out to his assistant and asked her where the other shoe was. The assistant then responded that she had no idea where the shoe came from because it came in a package with no return address and no note. Four days later, the sales person called to speak with the CEO, and when the assistant asked who was calling he said, "Just tell him the man with the other shoe is on the phone." Needless to say, the CEO picked up the phone immediately.

The salesperson then explained to the CEO that he had the other shoe and welcomed the opportunity to bring it to him. In return for delivering the gift, he asked that the executive invest 30 minutes with him so that he could ask a few questions to determine if he could be of assistance to the CEO's company as well. The executive eagerly accepted the appointment and stated that he appreciated the salesperson's ingenuity. It's interesting that someone who receives the pay of an executive was so excited about a pair of running shoes. It was the salesperson's creativity that really sparked this CEO's interest.

Another salesperson sent a lottery ticket attached to a note to top level executives. The note stated, "I am giving you a chance. Will you give me a chance to have a brief meeting to learn more about your vision for your company to determine if we can assist you in reaching your objectives?" She said this approach was very successful for her.

Yet another salesperson sent a small shoe filled with various types of chocolates in wrappers along with a note that stated, "Now that I have one foot in the door, please extend to me the opportunity of a quick meeting to explore how we may assist you and your organization." This idea landed the salesperson many more appointments as well.

I am not personally endorsing any of these techniques as ideas you should implement. These examples are only to illustrate the importance of being willing to take a chance and be different. Think outside of the box.

It is imperative to our success that we think out of the box and develop new and creative ideas to aid us in the pursuit of new opportunities.

As you read this you may think to yourself, "This is too gimmicky," or "That would never work in my territory," or "That is not my style," or "I have always done it this way and I am comfortable with it." Comfort is a difficult thing to risk, but only those who risk it have a shot at succeeding in a big way. In order to move forward today, you must be willing to adapt and try something different or new. Otherwise, your job will become monotonous and rather predictable. Keep in mind that the person you are calling on may have had fifty other sales professionals call on them recently. There has to be something that sets you apart. So get out of that rut. Move into the fast lane. Take a different route to get to your destination.

*"Two roads diverged in a wood, and I – I took the one less traveled by, and that has made all the difference."*
- Robert Frost

*"Don't be afraid to go out on a limb. That's where the fruit is."* - Anonymous

Another salesperson I trained used humor to his advantage. Every time I see Ralph, he has a new idea. On one visit to his company I asked him what was working for him recently. Ralph then stated that he had stumbled on a funny technique that was very successful for him. He went on to explain that after he had made at least seven attempts to reach the decision maker by telephone he would then leave this message:

> "Yes, Mr. Thompson. This is Ralph Johnson with XYZ Company again. I have left several messages for you and have yet to be able to reach you. I have also not heard back from you, so I guess it's safe to assume that you're not interested in our services. Mr. Thompson, I am fine with the fact that you have no need for our services, but after

trying to reach you so many times and never having spoken with you, I am now concerned. Therefore, Mr. Thompson, I would appreciate it if you would just call me back so that I will know that you're OK."

Ralph said that he would get return calls after this message and the decision maker would be laughing.

*"One mediocre idea you use beats ten mediocre ideas in your head."*
- Unknown

### Selling as a Science

Selling is also a science because it is based on discipline and logic. As a matter of fact, there is a formula for success.

*Calls = Presentations = Proposals = Sales = Income*

There is no way around it. If you want to make more income, you have to make more calls or contacts. If you make more calls, you will get more presentations. If you give more presentations, you will have proposals in which the client is willing to spend more for the solutions identified in the proposal. The more proposals you submit based on presentations, the more sales you will win.

It all starts with contacting a prospect. The most basic form of prospecting is the "cold call." This is when you make a phone call or personal visit to an organization with no prior relationship or contact. Most salespersons dread the cold call. However, once you learn to master the skill and fear of this technique, it can and will become the greatest tool in your sales toolbox for consistent success in selling.

Oh, by the way, if you ever feel as though you are making too much money, then reduce the number of calls or contacts you make. You will find that you are giving fewer presentations, and submitting fewer proposals. With fewer proposals, you will win fewer sales, thus accomplishing your goal of making less income.

It is impossible to get more heat from the stove (or fireplace) unless you put more wood in it first.

***Tears will get you sympathy, Sweat will get you results.***

Sales professionals have been trying for decades to a find a way to win more sales without making the calls. I constantly get asked, "Isn't there some other way to get sales without cold calls." There is one definite, consistent way to get more sales without cold calls. We will discuss this in a later chapter. There is an old saying about fighting that is relevant to this topic of cold calls:

***"It doesn't matter how great the technology you are fighting with, you will eventually have to send in ground troops to win any war."***

Likewise, all sales professionals eventually have to prospect to gain sales.

I have found that the majority of sales professionals don't know their sales ratios. For example do you know the following information about yourself?

- How many calls do you have to make to get an appointment?
- How many proposals do you usually need to submit to get a sale?
- Of the proposals you submitted, how many did you provide a presentation to?

If you perform an evaluation, you will find that you closed more of the sales in which you gave a presentation. You will also find the margins and commissions were higher on those sales. Once you identify the answer to the second question, you have determined your closing ratio. Therefore, if you submit four proposals and get one sale, your closing ratio is 25%. If your quota is $1 million dollars, and closing ratio is 25%, you must have $4 million working to close $1 million and reach your quota.

I often encounter salespersons whose goals for example are $1 million, and they may have a $1 million proposal already submitted. This is the only real opportunity they have on their sales forecast. Therefore, they put all of their eggs in that one basket hoping against hope that they win that project and meet their goal. They are desperate to win that sale because they have so much riding on it. Sometimes they may discount their product or services more than they should to ensure that they win the opportunity. They win it, but make no money.

That is why it is important to have many opportunities working. If their closing rate is 25%, the odds are against them winning that project and hitting their goal.

**The Importance of the Presentation**

The more presentations you give, the more sales you win at higher margins. You may avoid presentations because you don't like the exposure of presenting to strangers. Your boss may be present and you could make mistakes and expose your shortcomings. Or you may feel that you are being judged by your audience. You may prefer to send a proposal with some nice looking brochures. In your mind, you might consider that exercise to be a more efficient use of everybody's time, one that definitely minimizes your exposure to a potentially embarrassing experience.

Unfortunately, prospects or clients are more willing to invest in and pay more for your product or service when they get to see it, touch it, and compare it. You need to get as many of the client's senses involved in the buying process as possible.

I was talking to a sales team in one of my sessions about the importance of the presentation and the power it has in the buying process, and the Vice President of Sales confirmed my statements. She mentioned that at one time, she thought everyone who drove BMWs were "Yuppie Pond Scum." She drove an Acura at the time she harbored these feelings. Her lease on the Acura was about to expire when she went to a car dealership that sold both Acuras and BMWs. She had every intention of leasing another Acura. The salesperson mentioned that they had a new model BMW that was created with executives like herself in mind, and suggested that she consider a test drive. She abruptly stated, "I hate BMWs and the people who drive them."

The salesperson paused, and then calmly responded, "That is exactly why you would be perfect for a test drive. You will be able to provide us with an unbiased opinion on the BMW, and it will give you something to compare to the Acura just to confirm that it is the vehicle that is still best suited for you. We only need to drive it for five minutes or so. Can we take it for a quick ride?" "Okay, we can take it for a ride, but you are wasting my time and yours," she replied.

Her opinion quickly changed once she got behind the wheel. "Once I sat in the driver's seat, I felt like it embraced me. Then when I turned the ignition, I heard that powerful engine purr. I turned into oncoming traffic and had to accelerate quickly, and that vehicle went from 0 to 60 mph in 6.4 seconds. I had now become the thing that I hated: I was now Yuppie Pond Scum."

BMW is now the only brand of vehicle she purchases. But suppose the salesperson gave this response instead, "I understand that you are not interested in a test drive. Here is a brochure on the car, and maybe you can read it in your spare time, and let us know what you think the next time you stop by." Chances are she would still be driving an Acura.

As noted in this example, your odds are greatly increased in winning a new customer if you can get them physically and emotionally involved with your product or service. It is important to allow the prospect to participate as much as possible: if they can drive it, let them drive it. If they can open it, let them open it. If they can turn it on or off, let them turn it on or off.

**Selling as a Career**

The profession of selling allows professionally motivated high achievers to earn one the highest income levels in the professional world. There are sales professionals in every industry that have the same earning potential as doctors, professional athletes, successful entrepreneurs, etc. In order to achieve that type of success, you must consider what you need to do to make it a career, and not just a job. People who work at a job in most cases will have set hours that they work. They will work from 9 a.m. to 5 p.m., or 3 p.m. to 11 p.m. As a rule, they will only put in the time required to complete their prescribed work hours or tasks. They get out of their job exactly what they put into it. On the other hand, the most successful people in any occupation put in more time than is expected. They are willing to put in the time to be the best that they can be.

They become a lifetime student of their profession. I find it interesting that most professions other than sales require the workers in that field to get CEUs (continuing education units). On an annual basis, they must take classes in order to get better at what they do; hone their skills. They must continually increase their knowledge in order to bring added-value to the clients they serve.

However, I often work with salespersons that have been selling for five years to 35 years that feel they know all that they need to know. They see no reason to attend sales workshops or read books on the topic. The sales profession is not static. If you are not growing, you are dying. If you are not getting better, you are getting worse.

I believe that you should read at least one book per month relative to your profession to stay competitive. Napoleon Hill, a well-known author and inspirational speaker, identified in his tape series appropriately titled, "Lead the Field," that if you read 15 minutes per day, you can read two 150 page books per month. Therefore, reading eight minutes per day, you can read one book per month, which can help you compete more effectively. Remember, your customers no longer buy from you primarily because of what you sell. They now buy from you because of what you know and the added-value you bring.

CHAPTER THREE

# Time and Territory Management
# Do It Now!

One of the greatest struggles for most people is time management. Another problem for the average salesperson is procrastination. Procrastination is to the sales professional what kryptonite is to Superman. Remember in the comic books and movies how invincible Superman was until he was exposed to that mineral? Once exposed to kryptonite, he became ineffective and as weak as any other human. As long as he stayed away from that perilous kryptonite, he was unstoppable. So it is with sales professionals. The world, unrivaled success, wealth and/or peace of mind would be theirs if they would just stay away from their kryptonite - procrastination. Tomorrow is the busiest day of the week based upon what everyone plans on doing when tomorrow comes. Let's begin by exploring time management.

## Are You Managing Your Time?

I have a workshop with a segment on time management. Normally, most of the participants express an interest in this subject. Many of the workshop evaluations indicate that the participants wished that we had invested more time on this topic. In reality, more time invested on the subject would not help them. Execution of the topics discussed would help them immensely.

## Elevate Your Problem Clients or Fire Them

I know that recommendation seems harsh. However, problem clients prove to be the biggest hindrance for sales professionals.

They (sales professionals) have developed a clientele that always has a "fire to extinguish," gives them unrealistic deadlines for projects, increases their level of stress significantly, with the revenue dollars being minimal, or nonexistent. This problem starts at the beginning of the relationship. Usually, this occurs when you are trying to win business from the client for the first time.

The prospect says, "When can you deliver the _____ (you fill in the blank) to us?" The proper reply should be, "When do you need it?" or "What date do you absolutely need to have it by?" Instead, we respond by saying, "Tomorrow," or "In three days," or some other response that is unrealistic, and strain ourselves and our company's resources. The prospect or client is thinking to himself, "Wow, everyone else said that it would take at least a week. If they can turn things around that fast, I don't have to give them much notice at all." This could signify the beginning of a difficult customer relationship. You then go to your management and tell them, "The customer said they absolutely have to have it by this date" (which you actually committed your organization to).

I am not saying that you shouldn't jump through hoops to support a customer. I am saying that the fire you help put out should be the exception and not the rule. After you help put out the fire, have a conversation with the client to identify how as a team you can prevent the fire from ever starting. It's one thing to have one client like this. But what if you have a client list of 30, 60, 100 or even more clients that you have allowed or trained to expect you to be a miracle worker all day, every day? If the majority of your clients treat you like this, you are the problem. You created this problem. The good news is that you can also fix the problem. (We will cover how to solve this issue later in the chapter.)

Let's continue on with the premise that you agreed to a difficult timeframe. Now all of your resources or your support teams have to jump through hoops to fulfill an unrealistic commitment you made for the organization. Working under these circumstances may cause the quality of the work to be diminished due to inaccuracy or error issues, fatigue, or stress. Therefore, it may not meet the expectations of the prospect or client (p/c) even if you get your product or service delivered on time.

How many times have you stayed at work late, or gotten to work early, sacrificed family time, missed meals, or lost sleep in order to get a proposal prepared that was so pressing for the client? You delivered the proposal to the p/c at the time you committed, only to have it sit on their desk for a week, a month or longer before they review it and get back to you with a response.

**What is Your Time Worth?**

In many instances, we do the things we do because we have no idea of what our time is worth. We find ourselves investing the most time in the activities that provide the least return. At the same time, performing these tasks makes us feel that we are busy. My income doubled, and then tripled once I realized that I should invest my time where I get the greatest return.

Although I knew that time is money, and lost time is lost money that you can never ever get back, it became very obvious to me after a brief conversation with my financial advisor.

It was a bright Saturday morning and I was concluding a conversation with my financial advisor.

Advisor:   "So, what are you going to do now?"

Me:    "I am going to cut the lawn" (My home at the time was on a half-acre with plenty of shrubs to trim, sidewalks to edge, and weeds to pull).

Advisor:    "Tye, do you enjoy cutting your grass and working in your lawn?"

Me:    "Actually, I don't enjoy it at all."

Advisor:    Do you know what your time is worth per hour?"

Me:    "Of course I do."

Advisor:    "How much?"

Me:    (I told him the amount.)

Advisor:    "How long does it typically take you to do your lawn care?"

Me:    "About three hours."

He had me do the math and I realized that I was investing between 12 to 16 hours per month doing something that I didn't enjoy and that provided no return for the time I invested. I was busy, but not busy generating income or at least even getting a sense of enjoyment in return. I was busy with busy work. Based on what my time was worth, my lawn was costing me thousands of dollars per month and tens of thousands of dollars per year. That was time and money that I could never get back.

I then went on to realize that I spent additional time cleaning the pool, testing the water, and going to the pool store to get supplies, in an endless quest to keep it clean, pH-balanced, and algae-free. The pool took to one to four hours of my time per month.

I also washed and waxed our vehicles in an effort to save money, not realizing that the time I spent washing, waxing, and driving the car somewhere to be vacuumed consumed another two to six hours per month.

I then found that cleaning the house required a couple of hours per week. Not to mention home maintenance and repairs. How often does it happen that you start a home repair in an attempt to save money, and it takes more time than you expected, more aggravation than you anticipated, and in the end, you still have to call a professional to do or complete the job.

I ultimately turned all of the tasks mentioned above over to professionals that had better skills, knowledge, and equipment to get the job done.

This allowed me to:
- Spend more quality time with my family (priceless)
- Contribute back to my community with volunteer work (I helped those that could benefit from my knowledge or skills, creating goodwill, contacts, and networking opportunities)
- Conduct coaching sessions with students (generates revenue)
- Review potential investment opportunities (generates revenue)
- Work on writing this book (helps others, generates revenue)
- Send proposals and marketing materials to prospective clients (generates revenue)

Although paying someone else to do tasks that previously consumed my time cost me several hundred dollars per month, my income increased exponentially because I was able to use that time to grow my business by investing my time more productively. I had more time and money with less stress. I took the same approach with my work day. The things that had kept me busy during the workday, but did nothing to grow my business, became secondary. I made sure that the things I did first everyday grew the business. After that, I completed the busy work.

This is the issue you may be facing now. You do plenty of work every day, from dawn to dusk. You are busy all day. You may not even take a lunch break. But how much of your work went directly to generating a sale, a new client, or additional revenue in some way? You may be doing things on a daily basis that you should either make secondary chores or even delegate to someone else. You must realize what your skills are and how much your time is worth and begin to do the things that generate revenue first.

Now, let's identify what your time is worth.

## How Much is Your Time Worth?

Identify what your income goal is for the year: $_____

Divide your income goal by 50 weeks: $_____

Divide your weekly income by the number of selling hours available to you per week (usually 40 hours): $_____

(This final figure tells you what your selling hour is worth.)

Your selling hour should be the gauge by which you determine how to invest your time.

I once counseled a salesperson who was attempting to close a sale with an account. He stated that he had been pursuing the account for several months, and had invested an exorbitant amount of man-hours in that pursuit, including the proposal, follow-up, making revisions to drawings and proposals, and dropping off samples to this prospect. He felt the prospect was possibly playing him against his competition. I asked him what his income would be if he was awarded the sale. The commission would be approximately $2,500.

He did not know what his time was worth; therefore, we did the calculations on the previous page. We determined that he had invested almost $4,800 of his time chasing a $2,500 commission opportunity. He felt that he could not afford to walk away from the opportunity based upon the effort he had extended in pursuing the opportunity. To the contrary, I believed that he could not afford to waste his time any further with this opportunity. My belief is that he needed to get the client to make a decision. In too many instances, sales professionals attempt to create friends instead of customers. They operate a for-profit business that they treat like a not-for-profit operation.

Now that you know what your time is worth, let's examine how much you lose.

## How Much Do You Lose?

Your time is worth $_____ per hour.

_____ How many hours /week do you spend traveling in your territory?

_____ How many hours/week do you spend in non-prospect meetings?

_____ How many hours/week do you spend at your office (between selling hours of 8:00 and 5:00)?

_____ How many hours/week do you spend on personal errands, telephone calls, etc.

_____ How many hours do you waste per week by failing to plan and schedule?

_____ Total hours

_____ Total x your $_____ per hour = $ _____ lost per week

Multiply $ lost per week x 50 weeks (assuming you have two of weeks vacation. The final amount is what you lose per year.

$_____ lost per week x 50 weeks = $ _____ lost per year.

When I perform this exercise in my workshops, the amount of money lost by workshop participants normally ranges from $30,000 to as much as $165,000. I won't ask you to multiply the money you lose in a year by the number of years you have mismanaged your time, because I did not provide a nausea bag with this book. If you are courageous enough to perform this exercise, you may find that you have lost hundreds of thousands of dollars over the years, money that you could have used for:

- An education fund for your children
- Eliminating outstanding debt
- Making investments
- Making charitable donations
- Remodeling your home
- Purchasing a vacation home
- Going on fabulous vacations
- Enhancing your retirement account
- Helping out parents or family members

The list could go on. The bottom line is the that money that you lose because of mismanaging your time can never be regained.

## Painful Activities Versus Painless Activities

The majority of the successful people I have met have learned to do the painful activities first. The painful things are things you may not necessarily enjoy doing, yet they generate revenue. The key to success is doing the painful task on a regular basis. Painless things are the tasks that you may not mind performing; however, they do little to generate revenue.

Painful activities include (but are not limited to):

- Telephoning prospects for appointments
- Calling on accounts without prior contact or relationship
- Calling on difficult accounts
- Calling on problem accounts

On the other hand, painless activities include (but are not limited to):

- Reading and responding to e-mails
- Filling out reports
- Organizing your desk or files
- Calling on current customers that are friendly (but not in a purchasing mode)
- Office meetings

## How to Get Organized

Getting organized is simple. Staying organized is difficult. The steps for successfully managing your time are critical.

## Plan Your Day and Work Your Plan

A successful day, week, month, quarter, year, or life begins with a plan.

Let's start with your day. Plan your day the night before at the very latest. Write down the things you want to accomplish the next day. Once you have created your list, place the tasks in priority of importance, with #1 being the most important, and #10 being the least important.

The next day begins with the first task on your list. Don't move on to another task until you have completed the one you started. Many of you may be thinking, "In my industry or with my particular job, it is impossible to start something and finish it without being interrupted by important issues that need my immediate attention during the day." You can add another task to your list, or change the task priorities, but do not go to another task until you have completed the one that you are currently addressing.

You will be absolutely amazed how many more tasks you can complete each day when you train yourself to focus your energy on one task at a time. If you don't focus on one task at a time, you will continue to be scattered, changing course continually, and will have completed nothing by the end of the day.

I am not a scientist by any stretch of the imagination, but I do know that there is a huge difference between a flashlight beam and a laser beam. The flashlight beam is scattered and covers a larger area, while a laser beam is so focused that it can cut through steel. Recently, I read in an article that an office worker encounters 25 to 40 disruptions per day on average.

Each disruption required three to five minutes of a person's attention. This could equate to over three hours of time eroded from the job of accomplishing the tasks at hand, if we allow it.

Co-workers will also take up your time with things that are totally irrelevant to accomplishing the tasks at hand. You have to learn to say "No" to time-wasters.

A young lady that I coached was disturbed by how much money she had lost when we did the "How much do you lose?" exercise. She determined what her time was worth down to the minute. Therefore, whenever someone approached her to talk about things that had no relevance to the task-at-hand or to business, she would schedule time to talk with them at lunch or after-hours. She also realized that, in many instances, they wanted to gossip about another co-worker, or about things that would detract from the goals she was pursuing.

By becoming more focused, she increased her income by $50,000 in one year. She "worked her plan," and refused to be sidetracked.

**Managing Your Territory**

Another area that can erode your earning potential is that of poor territory management.

Tom starts his day at his office at site A. Tom has an appointment at site B. He concludes the meeting and has to drop off a sample to site C. Tom's next appointment is site D. He then goes to site E to make a courtesy call on a customer. Tom returns to his office (site A) after the courtesy call. Tom is what I call a "Star Salesperson." In this case being a star salesperson is not positive. He is a star salesperson because he did not manage his territory well on this particular day. Tom basically did a trip around the world in this territory. As you review the map of Tom's territory, you can see that based on his points of contact, he literally created a "star" in his territory. He allowed too much windshield time, which ate up a large portion of his day. Tom felt busy because he was away from the office all day and made a few sales calls.

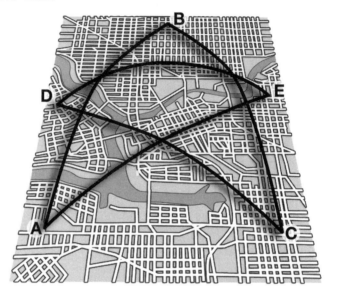

**Figure 2: Manage your territory more efficiently.**

There is a better way.

The most efficient way to manage your territory is to establish zones. For example, you may want to separate your territory into four zones (see Figure 3).

Next, identify the PTC (propensity to consume) index for each zone. This helps you to identify the potential for sales opportunities in each area. Armed with this information, you know where to invest your time based upon the areas that will provide you the greatest return for your time invested. The total opportunity or

PTC may look like this for your territory:

Zone A provides 50% of the revenue potential

Zone B provides 20% of the revenue potential

Zone C provides 20% of the revenue potential

Zone D provides 10% of the revenue potential

**Figure 3: Identify the PTC (propensity to consume) by zone.**

Now, determine how much time you will invest in each territory based on the potential for return. For example, there are 22 working days in the average month. You may choose Monday as an office day solely for administrative duties. This leaves you with 18 days per month to work your territory.

Since Zone A has the potential to provide 50% percent of the revenue, invest 50% of your time in that area. Look at your calendar and choose nine days this month that you will devote to cultivating opportunities in this area. Zones B and C each have the potential for 20% of the revenue, so select four days during the month to focus on each of these areas. Zone D would get one day per month.

| SUNDAY | MONDAY | TUESDAY | WEDNESDAY | THURSDAY | FRIDAY | SATURDAY |
|---|---|---|---|---|---|---|
|  |  | 1 ZONE A | 2 ZONE A | 3 ZONE A | 4 ZONE B | 5 |
| 6 | 7 OFFICE DAY | 8 ZONE A | 9 ZONE A | 10 ZONE D | 11 ZONE B | 12 |
| 13 | 14 OFFICE DAY | 15 ZONE A | 16 ZONE A | 17 ZONE C | 18 ZONE B | 19 |
| 20 | 21 OFFICE DAY | 22 ZONE A | 23 ZONE A | 24 ZONE C | 25 ZONE B | 26 |
| 27 | 28 OFFICE DAY | 29 ZONE C | 30 ZONE C | 31 ZONE B |  |  |

Figure 4: Schedule appointments by zone.

The key is to schedule appointments and tasks in the same zone on a given day. For example, suppose you are scheduling appointments for the 16th of the month and you are working in Zone A on that particular day. However, ABC Company from Zone C wants you to see them also on the 16th. The best thing to do is to schedule ABC Company for the 17th when you are going to be working in Zone C. Obviously, there will be occasions where you will need to see ABC Company on the 16th because of the magnitude or timing of the opportunity. However, my preference would be for you to exchange the entire day for each zone. In other words, schedule all of your appointments and tasks for Zone C on the 16th and all of your appointments and tasks for Zone A on the 17th. This takes tremendous discipline but the payoff is huge. You will find that most of your prospects and customers (p/c's) will be more respectful of your time when they observe that you are conscientious of your time. You will also find that you will see more p/c's daily, complete more tasks, and have less stress as a result of refusing to be a "Star Salesperson."

CHAPTER FOUR

# Effective Goal Setting

At the beginning of every year, my wife and I sit down and identify our goals and objectives for the year. It is a very exciting time for us. We set the game plan and steps we need to do to achieve our goals and the dates by which we want the goals accomplished. We are usually successful in accomplishing the majority of our goals. I have noticed that the goals we accomplish are not only the ones we were excited about, but they were also the ones in which we executed the game plan we established. The goals that we were unsuccessful on were the ones that we had developed a game plan and action steps for, but failed to execute.

That seems to be the case for most people who have great ideas and plans that never seem to come to fruition. They keep waiting for the perfect conditions or perfect timing; yet those conditions or times never come. I read a quote from General Douglas MacArthur that helped me to change my thinking. He said, "A decent plan violently executed today is far better than a perfect plan carried out next week." What a revelation! Our plan may appear inadequate or incomplete, but we should move forward anyway. If we wait until next week when we feel we have the ideal plan, the scenery will have changed, and our perfect plan is still not perfect. Don't just keep tweaking your plan and never start it. Work on your plan as you are carrying it out. I can't begin to count the great ideas that I have given birth to and never acted upon, only to see years later that someone else implemented the idea and reaped the rewards.

Failing to accomplish your goals is not as critical as not having a goal to pursue. A famous speaker and writer once said, "Success is the progressive realization of a worthy goal." If you establish goals and make steady progress towards the achievement of those goals, you are successful. It doesn't matter how fast or slow you progress, nor does it matter how large or small the goal is; the key is to move towards the goal.

There are two words we need to define before we move forward: *objectives and goals.*

An *objective* is an achievement, plateau, or gain that you aim for. Most of us mistake an objective for a goal. I often hear people say, "I want a new house," or "I want a new car," or "I want to make a lot of money." These statements by themselves are only wishes, hopes and, in some cases, pipe dreams.

On the other hand, a *goal* is an objective that you strive to attain within a specific time frame using a specific game plan. In order for the "I want a new house" statement to be a goal, you must be able to answer the following questions:

1. What are some of the characteristics/amenities of the home?
2. How many bedrooms, bathrooms, etc?
3. How many square feet will it have?
4. Where will it be located?
5. How much land will it be located on?
6. How much will it cost?
7. How much money will you need for a down payment?
8. How will you acquire the down payment?
9. When will you have the down payment?
10. What will be the amount of your mortgage payments?
11. What is your desired move in date?

You have clearly identified a goal when you have answered these questions.

For the record, anything you want to accomplish or acquire without a specific plan and timeframe is an objective.

There is something absolutely astounding about the impact of thinking through your goals, writing them down, and keeping them before you. This act unleashes creativity and tenacity that is unparalleled.

## Rules for Effective Goal Setting

Let's look at some of the guidelines for establishing effective goals:
- Must be written
- Must be specific
- Must be believable
- Review goals regularly
- START NOW!!!

## The Language of Goals

Not only is it important that we write down our goals, it is equally important to be mindful of what we write in establishing our goals.

The first assignment my clients receive when we begin coaching sessions is for them to write down their goals. I explain that it is critical that they be as specific as possible.

Denise was a new client, and she received this assignment as well. As usual, I gave her two weeks to complete the goal worksheet and return it to me. She set herself up for failure with her choice of words. Her first goal was:

> "It would be nice if I could possibly have a two or three bedroom condominium on or near the water in the next three to five years."

This goal was a pipe dream. Don't get me wrong: there is an outside chance she could get lucky and attain that goal. The chances were slim. Just as the company we keep impacts us greatly, so do the words we use. Denise restated her goal to read:

> "I will purchase a 3 bedroom, 2 bathroom condominium with a view of the water by December 31, 2004."

The first thing we must do to get started in goal setting is to identify the goals we want to accomplish. You may not be able to complete this in one sitting. Take a sheet of paper and begin to write down the things you want to accomplish. Don't focus on a particular order right now. Just get your thoughts on paper. Once you have your goals on paper, leave your list alone for one or two days. Then revisit your list and establish a priority to your goals. Select between 5 to 10 realistic goals that can be accomplished in the year, quarter, etc.

The next step is to prioritize your goals. We must now determine the goals we want to pursue first. The best way that I have seen to accomplish this was in the book, "The On-Purpose Person." The author used the tournament process for establishing the priority of goals.

Pull out your goal list, and sequentially number each goal. Advance number one to the next round by writing it down in the space to the right that's between numbers one and two. Now, choose between numbers three and four.

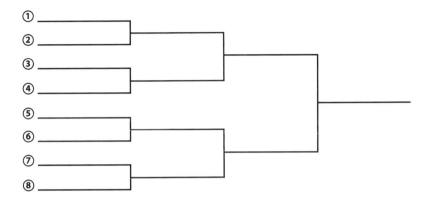

## The Secret to Hitting Your Goal: Don't Focus On It!

Now it's time to get started pursuing our goals. I have noticed some similarity between "hitting your targets" in life and "hitting your targets" with a target pistol. I enjoy bull's-eye target shooting, and the principles to being an effective target shooter also apply to accomplishing your goals in life. Let me explain: when shooting a traditional pistol, there are two sights - the front sight and the rear sight, as illustrated below:

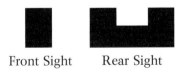

Front Sight     Rear Sight

The objective is to align the front sight in the center of the rear sight to achieve the proper "sight picture" below:

Your front sight must be aligned with the target, and the target should appear to sit on top of the front sight, as shown below:

The following is how it breaks down:

• The rear sight represents your game plan.

• The front sight represents your execution of the game plan.

• The target represents the goal you want to achieve.

As strange as this may seem, the key to successfully hitting the target is to focus on the front sight, not the target. As a matter of fact, the target should look blurry, and the front sight should be in focus. It is impossible for both the front sight and the target to be in focus at the same time. If the target is in focus, you will probably miss it. The key is to focus on the front sight.

Correct                    Incorrect

You are probably wondering, "What does this have to do with accomplishing my goals?" In order to achieve your goals, you must have a game plan. That game plan must contain action steps to be executed in a consistent manner or by certain deadlines. In many cases, we believe just establishing a goal will bring it to pass. Not so.

My wife and I wanted to acquire real estate property for investment purposes to hasten our long-term goal of retirement. We decided that we wanted to obtain two properties in one particular year: one property by June 30, and another by December 31. In order to accomplish this goal we developed the following game plan:
- Educate ourselves on real estate investing.
- Invest four hours per week researching/viewing properties.
- Make three offers per month on properties.

We had the goal written and the action steps identified. The only problem was that we did not execute the action steps. Therefore, at end of the year we had acquired no properties.

We were disappointed. The following year, we established the same goal and action steps. The only difference this time was that we executed the game plan. We were able to purchase two properties by August, because we focused on performing the activities necessary to accomplishing the goal. Our focus was not on the goal itself.

Take some time now to carefully consider how you are doing regarding achieving your goals. Make sure that you have a game plan and you are consistently performing the action steps in your game plan. Jim Rohn said "Goals. There's no telling what you can do when you get inspired by them. There's no telling what you can do when you believe in them. There's no telling what will happen when you act upon them."

CHAPTER FIVE

# Avoiding the Salesperson's Drive-by

Imagine that you have a 9:00 a.m. appointment with a client or prospect that lasts until 10:30 a.m. You conclude the meeting and head back to the office. There is nothing really pressing at the office, just some busy work you want to get busy with. You stop at a traffic light, and look to your left noticing a large building. You then think to yourself, "I wonder if there is an opportunity in that building that is waiting on me. I wonder if my next customer is in there. I wonder if someone in that building has a need for my products or services." As you ponder these thoughts, the light turns green and you drive off. A few months later, you are stopped at the same traffic light, and you notice that the building is still there. "One day, I am going to call on that building," you promise yourself. Six months later as you drive by the building, you notice your competitor's truck in front of the building, delivering the exact same product or service that you provide. This phenomenon is known as the Salesperson's Drive-By (SDB). I guess it is really not a phenomenon, because it is repeated millions of times per day by millions of salespersons. The SDB is different from the gang drive-by we now have throughout our society, where members of a gang drive-by in a vehicle and wound people. In the SDB, only the person driving gets wounded, along with his family, his company, etc. He is not taking advantage of chances to provide a worthwhile product or service to companies or individuals who may need what he provides.

I have gathered endless stories of the salespersons' drive-bys from around the country. I will share a few snapshots.

One of my clients was a company in a large stand-alone building in a complex of stand-alone buildings. Their sales professionals never prospected in the office park where their company was located. One day they saw their competitor's truck parked in front of the building next to their office. Upon seeing this, they quickly made their way over to the neighboring building and were able to get an audience with the primary decision-maker. The decision-maker said to them, "Oh, yes, you are our neighbors next door. We always wondered what you guys did."

I had another client who shared how a competitor sold a company that was one floor above them in their building a large amount of product. My client's sales professionals never considered prospecting the building in which they were located.

Another client shared a story with me that also illustrates the danger of the sales drive-by (or walk-by, in this case). He owns a company that sells office furniture. One of his salespeople made a call on a prospective customer whose offices were located in a five-story building. The prospect was leasing the top two floors of this building. The sales call went well; the salesperson concluded the call, got on the elevator, pressed the button for the first floor, left the building, got in his car, and drove back to his office.

Ultimately they won the business of the client on the fourth and fifth floors of the building. While they were installing their furniture on the top two floors for this customer, their competition was installing furniture for the bottom three floors. If my client's salesperson had initially made just another couple of calls in the building before he left to go back to his office, he may have sold five floors of furniture instead of just two floors. He will never know the outcome because he never made the calls.

We all probably have our own stories of sales drive-bys that we are trying to forget. Yet, many of us continue to do the same thing day after day. Insanity is defined as doing the same thing over and over again, but expecting a different result. Therefore, if we continue the same pattern (out of fear, laziness, etc.), we will continue to have the same result: missed opportunities, and lost income.

There is an old saying that "The best place to find your next customer is in your competition's backyard." Where do you think your competition will probably find their next customer? Why is it we feel that we must drive at least 15 to 20 blocks or at least thirty minutes away from our office before we can begin prospecting?

It is common to hear from sales professionals that "no one is purchasing products or services during a down economic period." They say clients have placed projects on hold, and budgets are frozen. The truth of the matter is that there are companies who are still purchasing during tough economies. They just aren't calling us.

Think about it: if all organizations stopped purchasing, the world economy would collapse in a matter of weeks, if not days. We choose to drive by these companies in hopes that our phones will ring. We decide to sit on the side of the road and wait for the storm to be over, and let them call us. Once they call us we are back in the bidding process.

I affectionately refer to individuals who wait for the telephone to ring as "Bid Jockeys." A bid jockey is a sales professional who is not proactive, but waits for the opportunities to come to him/her. They wait until the prospect realizes they have a need for their products or services. The prospect calls the bid jockey for a price and specifications. Now the bid jockey is in a race with all of the other bid jockeys. The race is normally to see who can get their price the lowest. And whoever wins the race really loses. The sale they win has margins/commissions so low that they will lose money if they make even the slightest miscalculations on the sale.

Yet, depending on the type of product or service sold, their time could be tied up for two to six months, or even longer. This limits their ability to find other and better opportunities. The bid jockey usually finds himself in a perpetual cycle of winning sales that have minimal payback and maximum work loads. Bid jockeys would also fall into the "Idler" category.

The salesperson that really prospers is proactive. They are "Drivers." They approach prospects who aren't aware that they have a problem yet. They make the prospect aware of the problem, get them sufficiently disturbed about the problem, and then show them how they can solve the problem. Drivers also help the prospect establish the criteria to which the bid jockey must respond or conform. The proactive salesperson or "Driver" understands the importance of getting into the prospect's office first or early.

Have you ever received a Bid package or Request for Proposal that perfectly fit the specifications of one of your competitor's products or services? Guess what? Your competition got to this account before you did. They have a greater chance of winning the sale *because they helped to establish the standard.*

I once worked with a client who was going through a tough period due to a recession. The salespersons were becoming negative and downtrodden because the phone no longer rang off the hook from customers desiring their services.

I told them that contrary to their current belief, companies were still spending money. They just weren't calling right then. I also told them that I could prove it.

We scheduled a cold-call blitz day. There were ten salespersons in this company and we developed ten teams by combining the salespersons with management and manufacturer's representatives from some of their suppliers. The goal of the cold call blitz was to:
   1. Get out and make new calls;
   2. Make as many new contacts as possible;
   3. Find new opportunities, and;
   4. Have fun.

By the end of the blitz day, the ten teams made a total of 247 new calls and uncovered 44 new opportunities. These were opportunities that they had been "driving-by" days earlier. The sales revenue that was ultimately generated from that one day of focused prospecting was enormous. One salesperson won a $713,000 sale, with a 27% margin, from that one day of prospecting!

## The Cure for the Drive-by

The cure I suggest is not to take two aspirin and call me in the morning. However, my cure does include the number two. Make two extra calls around each appointment you have scheduled. Make a call to the right and a call to the left of your appointment before you leave the building or the area. You may be in a situation where you are assigned only a handful of accounts. There may be 20 departments in one account and you are getting business from only five of those departments. You'll be amazed at the new opportunities you uncover.

Suppose for a moment that you average two appointments per day, and make an extra two calls around each appointment. The outcome would be:

$$2 \text{ extra calls x 2 appointments per day } = 4 \text{ extra calls/day}$$
$$4 \text{ extra calls per day x 5 days } = 20 \text{ extra calls/week}$$
$$20 \text{ extra calls per week x 50 weeks } = 1,000 \text{ extra calls/year}$$

You would make 1,000 extra calls in a year, just by making two calls around an appointment. Now, suppose for a moment you made an extra thousand calls in your marketplace over a year. Do you think you would find new business? I think we both know the answer is a resounding, "Absolutely!"

**Remember: The only difference between ordinary and extraordinary is that little extra.**

CHAPTER SIX

# The Essence of Questioning

Contrary to popular belief, the best sales professionals are not the ones with the ability to talk well and talk often. Truly, the most successful sales professionals are the individuals that have perfected the skill of asking deep, probing questions. The average salesperson talks way too much, especially when they first meet the prospect. They spend far more time sharing the following information:

1. Who they are
2. How great they are
3. Why they are great
4. How long they've been great
5. How long they plan on being great
6. Who else thinks they're great

The prospect/client (p/c) sits, bored stiff trying to figure out a way to signal their security officers to escort this salesperson from the building. In his book, "How to Win Friends, and Influence People," Dale Carnegie makes it clear that the best way to seem like a great conversationalist is to allow the other person to talk about themselves. They will think that you are the most intelligent and interesting person if you let them talk about themselves or their interests. The prospect/client doesn't want you to come in with your canned sales pitch and the briefcase full of brochures that you want to share with them.

You should strive to be a needs satisfier. A needs satisfier is someone who leaves behind all of their sales experience with other clients in the same industry of the prospect at that moment.

They eliminate all preconceived notions of what they think this client will like/need and what they would like to sell them. This sales professional literally goes into the call with an open mind.

The needs satisfier is like a doctor and the prospect is the patient. Now let's pretend for a moment your doctor tries a new approach with you one particular visit. You walk into the doctor's office for the first time, and sign in at the receptionist window. A nurse calls your name and asks you to come to one of the examining rooms.

After a few minutes, the doctor walks in with a cart full of medicine. He then says to you: "Hi, my name is Dr. Quack. Welcome to our clinic. We have been in this community now for 15 years and have served over 10,000 patients in the area. We have successfully treated many of our patients' illnesses. This cart holds many of the prescriptions we have provided to cure their ailments. Please listen carefully as I list the names of the medications.

 We have:

  Desquam-E 2.5 Emollient Gel
  Sulconazole Nitrate
  Crotamiton USP
  Mycostatin Cream
  Halobetasol Propionate
  Disulfiram
  Promethazine Hydrochloride
  Codeine Phosphate"

The doctor points to each medicine on the cart as he calls out the names and gives a brief description of what it does. He then asks you to choose a medicine for your visit. Most of us would be frightened by this type of approach from a doctor. We would consider the doctor to be unprofessional, and even dangerous. This doctor is prepared to provide a prescription based upon his/her experience and history with other patients, yet without clearly identifying the symptoms and the ultimate problem the current patient is experiencing. We would have very little faith in this doctor and rightfully so. However, there are a few of us that would find this approach somewhat adventurous. How could we possibly choose the proper prescription? Countless deaths occur each year because the wrong prescriptions are given to patients. How many dissatisfied customers do sales professionals create because we do not clearly understand the p/c's interests and issues?

I have no idea what the names of the medications above mean, nor do I fully understand their purpose. As a matter of fact, prospects and clients probably feel the same way when a salesperson begins spewing out industry terminology, jargon, buzz words, and acronyms.

Furthermore, countless sales and customer relationships are lost because many salespeople take the same approach to the customer or prospect as the doctor we just identified. There are too many instances in which sales professionals rely too heavily on their experience in working with other customers in a particular industry. They fail to ask the questions that uncover the customer's current circumstances, as well as the need driving those circumstances. The only way to truly identify the prospect/customer's needs is to ask deep, probing questions.

What really happens during a trip to the doctor's office? You sign in at the receptionist window. They give you a clip board with four or five pages on it. This is called your personal data sheet, or client information form. The office staff wants you to write down all of your personal information, including your address, phone numbers, insurance information, and medical history. Not only do they want your medical history, they want your family's medical history as well.

Basically, the doctor is doing his research on you before he meets with you. Once you've completed the personal data sheets, the nurse invites you to one of the examining rooms. In the examining room the nurse then takes your blood pressure, weighs you, and checks other vital signs. Now the doctor comes in. He will begin to ask some of the following questions:

"How are you today?"

"What seems to be the problem?"

"You say you feel dizzy. Tell me in your own words what this dizziness feels like."

"When does your dizziness occur?"

"How often does this occur?"

"What other symptoms have you experienced?"

The doctor may ask a number of other questions. He/she will also perform some additional examinations, prodding, poking, listening to your heartbeat, etc. The doctor may prescribe some medication if he/she feels that they have identified all of your symptoms and the underlying illness. If they are uncertain about the underlying illness, they may suggest additional tests as a means of determining the real issue at hand. Only then will the doctor give a prognosis and suggest corrective measures.

This is also the proper approach for the sales professional. We must ask questions to clarify the circumstances and understand the need behind the circumstances. We can provide the most appropriate solution only when we clearly understand the customer's situation.

**In order to sell John Smith what John Smith buys,**
**We must first see John Smith through John Smith's eyes.**

We must avoid the bad habit of prejudging based on history, our experiences, personal filters or preconceived notions.

Not long ago, I experienced a sharp recurring pain in my chest. It hurt every time I inhaled. This experience reminded me of a physical problem I had several years before called pleurisy. Pleurisy is the inflammation of the lining of the lungs. Because the pain felt identical, I believed I had pleurisy again. I called the doctor and explained to the nurse that I had pleurisy again and needed them to send in a prescription that would cure this illness. The doctor refused to send in a prescription until he physically examined me. I was a little perturbed that the doctor would waste my time and his when I knew that my diagnosis of the problem was accurate. Nevertheless, I made the appointment and went to see the doctor.

During my examination the doctor ran some tests, asked many questions, and did much probing and poking. His prognosis was different from mine. He determined that I had pulled a muscle in my chest, and every time I inhaled, the tight muscle was forced to stretch, causing the pain.

Amazingly, the symptoms for pleurisy and the pulled muscle were the same. However the cures were totally different. Pleurisy required an anti-inflammatory medicine, and the pulled muscle required a prescription for a muscle relaxer. Fortunately, the doctor did not trust my diagnosis. My solution would not have solved the problem.

How many times do you provide the wrong solution to a customer because they believed they knew what they needed for themselves? Ultimately, you are still held responsible for the wrong decision although you provided them exactly what they wanted. You should be held responsible because you are the expert, the professional. Therefore, you must not only pay attention to the symptoms, but also dig deeper to get to the real need that causes the symptoms.

You should refrain from proposing products and solutions until you have assessed and clearly understand the client's total situation.

## The Customer Needs Analysis

This process of uncovering p/c needs and wants is called the Customer Needs Analysis. The more thorough you are in this process, the easier the entire sales process becomes. This is the most important skill in the sales profession.

## Types of Questions

There are two types of questions that help us gain information from prospects or clients:
1. Open-ended questions
2. Closed-ended questions

## Open-Ended Questions

Open-ended questions are questions that cannot be answered with "Yes" or "No". These questions allow an interview to flow in a conversational way, and the client feels like they are in control because they are doing the majority of the talking. However, you actually navigate the conversation. You get more and better information by asking open-ended questions. Some examples of open-ended questions are:

"What is your vision for your company?"

"What are you currently doing to attract talented workers?"

"Why is it important for your company to expand now?"
"What would be the impact on your department if you don't reduce turnover?"

These questions cause the client to provide detailed information into their circumstances and needs which will allow you to provide more accurate and relevant solutions.

## Phrases Implying Need (PIN)

One of the major benefits of the open-ended question is that it is the only type of question that encourages the p/c to respond with phrases that imply a need. The p/c only has a need if they say they have a need. Phrases that imply a need resemble the following:
"We need to ...."
"We want to ...."
"We have to ...."
"It is critical that we ...."
"It is important for us to ...."
"We are interested in improving ...."

Train your ears to pick up on these clues when you hear them because the client will reveal exactly what you have to do or provide to earn their business. It always amazes me, in training sessions and in the field, how many times salespersons overlook these phrases that imply a need.

In one of my sales training workshops, we provide the participants with a case study on an organization. They will have an appointment with the decision maker to interview him/her and uncover their needs. We also record the participant's interview with a video camera so they can review it at a later time. They also receive an information sheet that reveals all of the information they could have received if they had picked up on the phrases that imply needs, and queried into each issue. Upon reviewing the video, the participants are amazed at how many clues the client gave them that they totally missed. Many identify the reason they did not pick up on the p/c's needs was that they had their own agenda. They were more concerned about asking the questions, not the answers given.

Effective questioning is like bowling. In bowling, the more pins you hit, the higher your score and the better your chances are of winning the game. In questioning, the more of the client's PINs you identify and hit, the more valuable you are in the eyes of the client and, thus, the greater your chances of earning their business.

This question uncovers the positive or negative effect an issue will have on the prospect based on whether they achieve or fail to accomplish the objective.

The impact/open-ended question is important to include in your line of questioning. I prefer to ask impact questions that predominantly identify negative impact versus positive results. In other words, if I ask 10 impact questions in an interview with a prospect, 8 out of the 10 impact questions will seek negative consequences. The reason for this is most people will respond or act faster to the fear of losing something than they do to the possibility of gaining something.

An example of this took place when my daughter was beginning college. I considered getting a cell phone for her and I visited several companies. Only a couple of the salespersons asked any questions regarding my desire to get the phone. I explained that I traveled extensively. That being said, I am away from home and my family quite often. Salesperson A stated: "Wouldn't it be great for your daughter to have a phone so she could keep in touch with you whenever she wanted so the two of you can maintain a strong relationship?" Although my daughter is precious to me, the lure of enhancing our relationship did not prompt me to buy a phone from that salesperson.

A couple of days later, I stopped by another store evaluating cell phones and service plans. Salesperson B probed into my circumstances regarding the need for a cell phone. Salesperson B stated: "Based on the time you are away from home, how important is it for your daughter to have a way to reach someone for help in the event of an emergency?"

The first thought that came to mind was my being on the other side of the country while my daughter is stuck on the side of the road in a broken-down vehicle. She has no way of calling anyone to assist her. She may even have to trust a stranger to assist her. Although that is not the picture the salesperson attempted to paint, that is the picture my mind conjured up. Needless to say, I purchased a phone that day from that salesperson.

Both salespersons did a great job of probing to understand my circumstances and needs. One salesperson attempted to appeal to positive aspects of the cell phone for my daughter. The other appealed to the negative aspects of my daughter not having the phone. The latter salesperson won.

There are two primary reasons customers don't purchase our product or services.
  1. They are not aware of a problem.
  2. If they are aware of the problem, they are not sufficiently disturbed by it.

It is the salesperson's job to make the customer aware of the problem and to help them to become sufficiently disturbed.

One day Joe, the salesperson, was preparing to leave his office to go on sales calls, when his manager said, "By the way, I am riding with you today." Joe mustered up a fake smile and said, "Great." Joe had no clear objectives for his appointments, nor did he do extensive questioning to identify the prospects' needs. He did the routine "Show up and throw up" approach. He talked endlessly about himself, his company, and the products. Needless to say, the calls did not go well.

It was a long ride back to the office at the end of the day. Then Joe said to himself, "If someone doesn't do something soon, someone is going to be in trouble." He then chuckled to himself and said to his manager, "Well you can lead a horse to water, but you can't make him drink." The manager then said, "Joe, you're right. It is not your job to make them drink; it is your job to make them thirsty. If you make them thirsty they will want to drink on their own."

Your prospects will buy your products or services because:
    1. They want it, or;
    2. They need it.

There are usually circumstances surrounding the purchase whether it is driven by a need or want. You serve your client better when you ask deep analytical questions to identify the real need behind the circumstance that is driving the need for your product or service. Provide them with a solution that meets the need more than the want. Your client will also spend more for your solution if you sell to the real need that is driving the circumstance.

Speaking of driving, a perfect example happened a few years ago. My wife and I were in the market for a new vehicle. She had recently survived a major accident which totally destroyed her vehicle. Fortunately, she walked away without a scratch. The only injury she sustained was minor swelling to both of her wrists because she tensed up in anticipation of the crash.

We wanted her to have another car just like the one she previously drove because the safety features built into the vehicle had minimized her injuries, and probably saved her life.

I went to the dealership, and a salesperson approached me. I told him that I was interested in a particular make and model. He did not ask any questions to understand why I was interested in that particular vehicle. The only thing that mattered to him was that I wanted to buy a car. Therefore, he sold to my circumstance of needing an automobile. He failed to sell to the need that was driving my desire for that particular vehicle.

We found the vehicle we wanted and we began haggling about the price. During our negotiations, he gave me several expensive concessions. Had he sold to my real need, he wouldn't have had to offer me those concessions. He did get the sale, however, he had to sacrifice his commissions and margins because he didn't know his customer.

On the hand, the sale could have been more profitable for him and his company. He could have gotten better information through better probing. He could have said to me the following:

"Mr. Maner, I can appreciate that a reduced price, the CD package, and tinted windows are things you want me to provide to you, and at no additional charge in order to earn your business."

"As I understand it, the real reason you are here today is to purchase a vehicle because your wife survived a major accident because of the safety components that are built into this vehicle."

> "Would you be willing to move forward today with this investment that will continue to provide your family with the safety they deserve even though it doesn't have the CD player and tinted windows?"

The circumstance was that I wanted a vehicle. The real need was an automobile that provided exceptional "Safety" and "Security" for my family. I will always pay more for that. I would have paid for the tinted windows, the CD player and would have accepted less of a discount if he would have sold to my real concern. But from the consumer's standpoint, why pay for it if the salesperson is willing to give it away for free.

## Probing Deep to Uncover Customer Needs

I usually find that the salespersons who pick up on phrases that imply needs fall into one of two categories. They are what I refer to as a Swimming Sally or a Scuba Sam. Sam has a much larger income and experiences greater success in selling than Sally. This has nothing to do with gender, but, has everything to do with how deep he is willing to dive into the customer's needs. Below are examples of both on a sales call.

## Swimming Sally

Sally:   "What are you looking for in a system?"

Client:   "We really want to have more flexibility in our next system."

Sally:   "We have exactly what you need. I propose the XYZ system, because it can ....."

## Scuba Sam

Sam: "What are you looking for in a new system?"

Client: "We really want to have more flexibility in our next system."

Sam: "Flexibility means different things to different people. Just to clarify, what do you mean when you say flexibility?"

Client: "By flexibility, I mean a system that is somewhat intuitive, and will adjust to the worker instead of our staff adapting to the system."

Sam: "I see, and why is the ability to adapt to the worker such an important issue for your company?"

Client: "We have three shifts working each day, and we want to minimize downtime and enhance worker performance."

Sam: "What do you feel will be the long-term value from a system that could provide this to your staff?"

Client: "This would drastically reduce our operating cost and improve our profit picture."

Sam: "I just want to make sure that I am clear on what you are looking for. You are looking for flexibility, which means you want a system that is intuitive and will adjust to the worker instead of the worker needing to adjust to the system. This is important because it will help minimize downtime and improve worker performance which will ultimately reduce your operating cost, thereby improving the company's profitability.  Did I get it right?"

Client:    "You sure did."

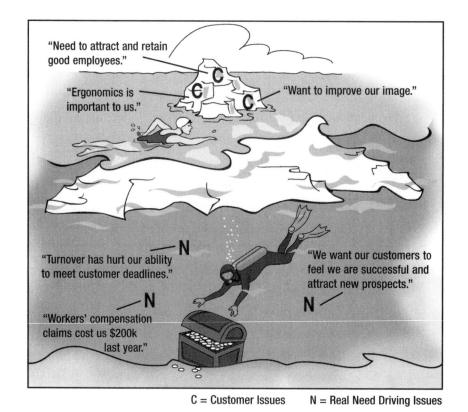

C = Customer Issues    N = Real Need Driving Issues

It is probably clear now why Sam is more successful than Sally. Sally asked one question and immediately came up with a solution without fully understanding the p/c's real need. Therefore, Sally is selling to a circumstance. As a rule, p/c's will spend less money to solve a circumstance.

On the other hand, Sam asked a question, identified a phrase that implied a need from the p/c. Sam put on his scuba gear and went deep to identify the real need that is driving the circumstance. As a rule, p/c's will invest more money to solve a need.

Now is the time for self analysis. Look at yourself and your style of questioning. Which salesperson do you most resemble, Sally or Sam? If the answer is Sally, you are in the majority of sales professionals. The good news is you can change starting today. If you most resemble Sam, congratulations, because you are in the top of your profession.

## The Advantages of Open-Ended Questions

There are several benefits to using open-ended questions in the customer needs analysis process. Both the p/c and the salesperson receive this value. Open ended questions:
- Shows sincere interest by salesperson;
- Allow the p/c to speak about something of great interest to them;
- Draw the p/c out;
- Get volumes of information;
- Get to real concerns and issues, and;
- Help to build rapport.

## Closed-Ended Questions

Closed-ended questions are questions that can be answered with "Yes" or "No," a response that provides a quantity, or a choice of alternatives that you provide. Some examples are:

"Do you have a budget established?"

"How many employees do you have currently?"

"Would you prefer the black or the burgundy ink pen?"

Do not ask many closed-ended questions in a row, or the client will feel as though they are being interrogated.

Closed-ended questions will help you get specific information, and are especially important for confirming our understanding of the customer's comments or needs. For example:

You:    "So, as I understand it, you are looking to improve morale in your company because that will help to reduce employee turnover, is that correct?"

Prospect:    "Yes, that is correct."

In that example, we found that we clearly understood the client. This type of question will also help identify when you misunderstood them or did not completely understand:

You:    "So, as I understand it, you are looking to improve morale in your company because that will help to reduce employee turnover, is that correct?"

Prospect:    "Yes, that is part of it."

You:    "I see. What part did I miss?"

Prospect:    "Well, although we feel higher morale will help minimize employee turnover, we also believe our employees will do a better job serving our customers."

Therefore it is critical that you conclude a series of questions with a closed-ended question to confirm your understanding of the clients needs before you move on to another topic.

A good series of combining open and closed-ended questions would resemble the following:

What are you looking for in a ...? (open)
Just to clarify my thinking, what do you mean by...? (open)

Why is that is so relevant for your company now? (open)
How many employees do you currently have? (closed)
Are you planning to increase staff this year? (closed)
What will happen if you aren't able to ... (impact/open)
As I understand it, you are ... (restate what you believe you
heard them say)... Is that correct? (confirming/closed)

Your client will appreciate your questioning because it indicates
that you are genuinely interested in them and their desires.

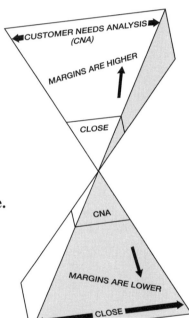

**The more thorough
you are in analyzing
the customer's needs,
the easier it is to close.**

The chart above illustrates two approaches to the customer needs
analysis. The top portion of the chart displays the most effective
approach to analyzing the needs of the p/c. Basically, it identifies
that the more thorough you are on the front portion of the sales
process in evaluating the needs of the p/c, the easier it will be to
close the sale on the back end of the process. You'll be perceived
as a business ally and someone that brings great value to their
organization. As a consequence, your margins and commissions
will be higher.

The lower portion of the chart identifies the exact opposite outcome and impression. The less time you invest uncovering the direction, goals and needs of the client, the more difficult it will be to close the sale. You will be perceived as a vendor, someone who is just concerned about making a sale. As a consequence, your margins and commissions will be lower.

Note in both approaches you invest the same amount of time in the sales process. Either you invest your time wisely on the front or spend your time inefficiently on the back end.

Remember this:
*A Vendor is a dime a dozen and takes up space,*
*A Business Ally is hard to find, and difficult to replace.*

CHAPTER SEVEN

# The Significance of Listening

Questioning and Listening are two sides of the same coin. They go hand in hand. You can't have one without the other.

Has this ever happened to you? You asked someone a question, and your mind drifted off to something else while they were answering your question. After they finished answering your question, you had no idea what they said. You were too embarrassed to ask them to repeat themselves because they would know that you weren't listening the first time they answered you.

You can ask the most brilliant and thought-provoking questions known to mankind, but if you aren't listening effectively, the questions are in vain.

This book covers many skills necessary for any sales professional to be consistently successful in the selling profession, but none is more important than effective listening. The problem stems from the fact that our computer-like brain processes information several times faster than we can receive it. The brain wants to race ahead and come to a conclusion so we can be more efficient with time. The only problem is that we are developing conclusions and our responses based on incomplete information and assumptions of what the person *might* say. This is a dangerous practice known as listening to respond.

## Listening to Respond

Listening to respond is a common practice. In communicating with customers, a spouse, a co-worker, a friend, our children, etc., you will hear the same statement or close to the same statement dozens of times over the period of that relationship. In some cases, you may hear the same statement hundreds or even thousands of times. Once you hear the first five or six words of that oh so familiar sentence, your brain registers that you have heard this statement hundreds of times before, so there is no real need to listen to the entire statement. You then cut them off in the middle of their sentence and respond or you stop listening to them and start formulating your response.

Although you have heard that statement a multitude of times, isn't is possible that the person speaking can change one word in that statement that changes the entire complexion of that statement?

I have a fun listening exercise that I conduct in my workshops to help assess how well or how poorly the participants listen. I make a statement and then ask the participants to write down the correct answer after they have carefully considered every aspect of my statement.

An example of a question that is asked in the exercise is:

How many animals of each species did Noah take aboard the ark with him during the great flood?

The most common response is "two."

That response is incorrect. The correct response is "zero." He didn't take any animals on during the flood; he took them on before the flood. The one word, "during" makes all the difference in this example.

One participant had heard a variation of this question. The variation is as follows:

How many animals of each species did Moses take aboard the ark with him?

The correct answer in this case is still "zero" because it was Noah, not Moses that took the animals aboard.

However, because he recognized the first few words in the question as being similar to what he had heard in the past. He then proceeded to correct me and informed me that I said the statement incorrectly. I then assured him that I was accurate in my delivery. But he was insistent that I was in error. Clearly, this participant was listening to respond.

Examine both questions and you'll notice similarities although they are quite different.

How many animals of each species did Noah take aboard the ark with him during the great flood?

How many animals of each species did Moses take aboard the ark with him?

Many participants write their answer before I complete asking the question. Needless to say their answer is usually incorrect.

They are able to laugh at themselves after the exercise when they see their failure to accurately answer simple questions. In reality, listening to respond is no laughing matter in real world scenarios.

## Listening to Understand

Listening to understand is totally different from listening to respond. Listening to understand means you are paying careful attention to the speaker and really trying to understand what he or she is saying or how they are feeling. Here are some rules for listening to understand effectively.

## Let the Speaker Speak

The prospect/client is often interrupted because the Salesperson believes that he has heard enough to determine what the p/c is thinking or going to say next. The listener proceeds to interrupt the prospect/client and attempt to complete their sentence or thought. The other thing that happens often is the salesperson attempts to provide a solution to the problem the p/c is identifying without fully understanding it. In both cases, the outcome can be negative. That being said, the listener must:

    A. Listen intently to every word the speaker is saying;

    B. Pay attention to voice inflection, and;

    C. Pay attention to facial expressions.

## Let Your Attention Show

One of the most frustrating things for a speaker is to not know for sure that the person(s) to whom he or she are speaking is paying him or her attention. The p/c feels discounted and that the listener is not genuinely interested in them or their concerns. The listener may seem more interested in their checkbook. The listener must:

    A. Provide good eye contact with p/c.

    B. Nod their head or use facial expressions periodically
       to show interest or comprehension.

C. Verbally show that they are paying attention by saying
   1. "Uh Huh."
   2. "I understand."
   3. "Really!"
   4. " I see."

## Take Notes

Have you ever participated in a meeting or telephone conversation, and been unable to remember certain details only minutes after the interaction. I am always concerned when I go to a restaurant either alone or with a group, and the server attempts to remember our orders without writing it down. Usually, something about our order is not correct. This is why it is so critical to take good notes. Contrary to popular belief, taking notes doesn't mean that you are not paying attention. It means that you are genuinely interested in the speaker and you want to remember what is being said and get it right.

I would normally say, "Mrs. Johnson, what you are sharing with me is very important to you and your company, therefore it is important to me, and I want to make sure I get it right. Do you mind if I take some notes?" The usual response is "Yes." I ask permission to take notes for a few reasons.

A. Some organizations have highly classified information (e.g. defense companies, software companies, military facilities, etc.), and I want it to be clear that I am taking notes on what they are saying, not what I may have seen in their organization.

B. It makes them aware of my attention to detail in my quest to address their needs.

    C. It also makes the speaker aware of other salespersons'
       lack of attention to details if they don't take notes.

## Concentrate

It is amazing how thoughts about everything in the world can occupy your brain while the prospect is sharing his thoughts with you. Thoughts may interrupt your concentration, such as:

    "Did I turn off the oven this morning?"
    "My vacation in Hawaii sure was great four years ago."
    "I need to pick up some dog food from the grocery store."
    "I didn't take anything out for dinner tonight."
    "I sure hope my next appointment goes well."

In many cases, you must mentally fight with yourself to stay focused. Nothing should be more important to you than the person sitting before you and what he or she is sharing with you.

You must clear your mind of all things that are not relevant to the conversation you are currently engaged in.

You will be amazed how much valuable information the client will provide you to help you earn or keep their business.

## Pay Attention to All of the Details

This relates back to listening to respond. Make sure you listen to every word, not just the first few words of the sentence.

## Pause Before You Respond

It is critical to pause after the p/c has finished speaking. You must carefully consider what they said, and determine the most appropriate response. Otherwise, it is likely that you may not have an accurate understanding of the p/c's commentary or question. In that case the answer given will be inappropriate or incomplete.

Remember, effective listening is more than just using your ears. It means using your eyes, your ears, your brain, and using the keys referenced in the previous pages to make sure you are listening to understand, not just to respond.

CHAPTER EIGHT

# The 30-Second Commercial

I often talk to sales professionals who have been in sales for 10, 15, 20, even 30 years. Many of them are extremely successful. I have seen these very successful individuals become almost tongue tied when someone catches them off guard with the question, "So, what do you do?" In some instances they have the "Deer in the Headlights" look. Their response is normally something like this, "Well, um, I, I mean we, well I sell copiers (or cars, cell phones, whatever the product or service is). "Oh, I see, how interesting," is the usual response. Unless the person that asked the question has an immediate need for your product or service, they typically try to make a hasty exit.

More often than you can probably imagine, sales professionals aren't able to adequately identify exactly what it is they do and how they bring value to individuals or organizations.

I conducted a workshop in Seattle. Very early in the morning I went down to the hotel lobby to meet the person who was going to give me a ride to the workshop I was conducting. As I got onto the elevator on the 38th floor, a couple got onto the elevator at the same time. They looked as though they'd had a rough evening. "Good Morning," they said in a fatigued voice. "Good Morning!" was my reply in an enthusiastic voice. The couple appeared surprised to hear someone so positive first thing in the morning. "What do you do?" was the man's response. "My name is Tye Maner, and I represent a training and consulting organization whose primary focus is to assist our clients in improving their profitability by enhancing the performance of their staff."

"We really need to talk to you," the woman responded in an excited tone. I quickly found out who they were and the company they worked for. They were married and owned a decent-sized organization. We exited the elevator on the lobby floor, exchanged cards, and scheduled an appointment to assess their needs. I found a new opportunity on a 20-second elevator ride. Maybe that is why the 30-Second Commercial is also referred to as the Elevator Speech. Within 90 days, I was doing business with this company.

Keep in mind that the 30-Second Commercial is a brief statement that communicates the following information:
- Who you are
- Who you represent
- What your company does
- How what your company does helps others
- Request permission for appointment (if appropriate)

The 30-Second Commercial is not the time to go into a laundry list of all the products and services you provide. More than anything your goal is to briefly identify the potential benefits of your products or services to your listener.

Suppose for a moment my commercial was like this:
"My name is Tye, and I represent Tye Maner & Associates. We are a training and consulting company, and we provide coaching to executives, managers, and salespeople alike. We also conduct workshops on the following topics, Successful Coaching and Managing, Leadership and Interpersonal Skills, Customer Service, Negotiations,

Presentation Skills, and general Sales Training courses. We also provide Keynote speeches on the following topics…"

Did your eyes begin to glaze over as you read the last example? Well, that is exactly what happens to most people who listen to that type of commercial.

I once read a statistic that in a particular year over twenty million 1/4-inch drill bits were sold in the United States. However, no one purchased the 1/4-inch drill bit because they wanted a 1/4-inch drill bit. They purchased the 1/4-inch drill bit because they wanted a 1/4-inch hole. That is exactly what you sell, the outcome not the product. Remember, anytime someone acquires your products or services, they are acquiring it for the result it will provide.

The reason for my initial success on the elevator was that I talked about the outcomes with which all executives or decision-makers are concerned, not the products or services. Those concerns are:
- Profitability
- Performance
- Perception

Those 3-Ps directly contribute to the ultimate success or failure of an organization.

## Profitability

Every organization strives for a great profit picture. There are many things that can adversely affect profitability. Decision-makers are concerned with anything that has a negative effect on the profitability of their organization. Some examples of business

issues that can have a negative impact are:
- Interest rates
- Level of unemployment
- State of the economy
- Changes in technology
- Changes in market demand ( customer buying habits)
- Loss of customer base
- Getting new products/services to market quicker
- Unmotivated workers

The list includes only a small amount of the issues that can hinder the profitability of companies. Organizations have control over some of the issues while some of them they don't. There are probably thousands of possible issues, if not millions. Regardless of what the concern is, it will probably fall into one of the 3-Ps.

**Performance**

The performance factor is one area that has a direct impact on the other two Ps. Performance issues can be relevant to:
- The overall organization
- A particular department/division
- An individual
- A process
- Equipment

Leaders naturally desire to improve performance. I personally do not know of any leader who is not immensely interested in getting better performance out of his staff and equipment.

**Perception**

Most companies are concerned about how they are perceived by:
- Customers/clients

- Suppliers
- Employees
- Stockholders
- Competitors
- The public at large

The other two Ps can be directly impacted by the wrong perception or a negative image in the eyes of any of the people above. For example, a salesperson's performance suffers when they feel less skilled or equipped than their competition, or that their product or service is inferior to other companies in their industry. This ultimately impacts profitability. Failure on your part to live up to your customer's expectations adversely affects their perception of your organization. Consequently, they will vote with their dollar, and do business with someone else, ultimately reducing your revenue and impacting profitability.

The 3-Ps are interconnected and affect each other both positively and negatively respectively.

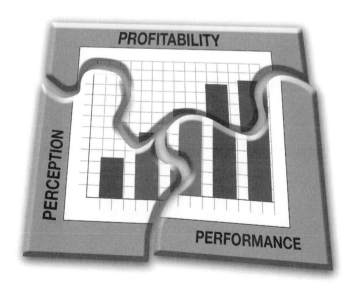

A good example of this is in another 30-Second Commercial. I once worked in the office furniture industry. Whenever I was asked what I did for a living, I would say, "I represent a research and design-driven manufacturing company named Herman Miller, and our primary focus is to help our clients get improved performance from their three greatest assets: their real estate, their people, and their technology."

"As a matter of fact, we provided a client with an idea that helped them get 25% more people into their current facility, which alleviated the need to lease additional space. That helped to improve their profit picture. I would like to schedule a brief appointment with you to learn more about your vision and direction for your company to determine how or if we can help you reach your objectives."

Did you notice that I didn't mention office furniture? That is because executives don't care about furniture. They also don't care about cell phones, copiers, long distance service, group health insurance plans, computers, advertising. They care about what your product or service will do for their organization, and how it will impact the 3-Ps.

The 30-Second Commercial works only if you perfect it and use it.

I recently received an e-mail from a manager sharing a success story. Stephanie, a session participant, agreed to put her new-found skills to use. The really exciting outcome from the session occurred when she attended a ground-breaking ceremony the following week for an out-of-town company building a new facility. By luck, Stephanie happened to stand next to the CEO & President of the company that was breaking ground. They began a conversation and Stephanie gave her 30-Second Commercial. The CEO was very impressed and agreed to a future appointment to discuss his vision for the new facility. Stephanie was amazed at how effective the technique was for getting the attention of the top decision-maker.

Now, develop your 30-Second Commercial.

## Your 30-Second Commercial

Briefly identify:
- Who you are
- Who you represent
- What your company does
- How does what your company does benefit others
- Request a brief appointment

Write your commercial below:

_____

_____

_____

_____

_____

_____

_____

_____

_____

_____

_____

_____

_____

_____

_____

_____

_____

_____

_____

_____

_____

_____

_____

_____

Take the commercial you just wrote and share it with other sales professionals whose opinion you trust to get their feedback. Share it with your manager for feedback. You may even share it with top level executives with whom you have a relationship. These individuals will give you valuable viewpoints to help you craft and fine tune your commercial.

Next, memorize your commercial. You should have it down to the point that if I were to awaken you in the middle of the night, and ask you to recite your commercial, you would be able to do it.

Once you have it completely memorized and can present it on a moment's notice, then you will be able to vary your commercial based on the occasion.

A first rate 30-Second Commercial will help you:
- Improve your confidence with initial contacts;
- Enhance you professional appearance, and;
- Concisely identify the value you bring to your clients.

# CHAPTER NINE

# Telephone Prospecting

One of the most important tools in the sales professional's tool kit is the telephone. First of all, you can make far more contacts using the telephone in 30 minutes than you can in driving around in the same amount of time. Secondly, the telephone allows you to secure definite appointments with a better qualified prospect at a time that is convenient for both of you.

As I said earlier, the only difference between ordinary and extraordinary is that little extra. The previous statement is true regarding telephone prospecting also. I have recommended for years to thousands of salespersons to make prospecting calls via telephone for 30 minutes per day. I also guaranteed them that if they did this every day plus make the two extra calls around each appointment, they will have more business than they could imagine. There were many who tried it to prove me wrong. To the contrary, they found my assertion to be quite accurate. Do the math.

30 minutes per day = 2.5 hours per week
= 10 hours per month
= 120 hours per year

That equates to 15 eight hour working days per year. Now imagine sitting at your desk for 15 consecutive days and doing absolutely nothing but making one call after another all day long with enthusiasm, confidence, and a conversational tone.

There is no doubt that you would find great opportunities. Many of those uncovered opportunities would convert to good customers and nicer commission checks. The only problem is we both know that you can't and won't sit down and make one phone call after another for 15 consecutive days. That is why we suggest you only call 30 minutes per day. That is easier to digest, and the outcome is the same.

## Plan Your Calling Time

The best approach is to plan who you are going to call prior to sitting down to make the calls. This allows you to maximize your calling time. It is also a good idea to determine when you are at your best. Some of us should make our calls first thing in the morning, while we are fresh. Others are best in the afternoon. We have an exercise in one of our workshops that require the participants to leave voice mails. The intent is to leave a voice mail that has an impact. The desired result is that the prospect will return your call right away, or accept your call when you call again.

As a part of an exercise in one of my classes, I ask the students to call my office and leave practice voice mails. One of my students decided to leave two voice mails just to see if one was more effective than the other. He left one message in the afternoon and another message first thing the next morning. The class listened to all of the voice mails they had left and gave each other feedback on each voice mail. John's first message was spectacular. He came across as conversational, confident, knowledgeable, and enthusiastic; someone with whom I'd like to do business. The message he left the following morning was the exact opposite. His voice was monotone, and unsure. He had no enthusiasm. I would not have returned his call or scheduled an appointment with him based on his second message.

## Seek Only the Appointment

The purpose of telephoning the decision-maker is to get an appointment (if you are an outside salesperson). Don't try to establish rapport over the phone initially. Get to the purpose of your call as soon as possible. To decision-makers, the telephone is usually seen as a disruption. The person you're calling is probably doing something else at the time of your call. Executives we surveyed said that they get agitated by sales professionals who call them with no prior relationship, and begin the conversation with, "Mr. Johnson, How are you today?" They think to themselves, "Listen, I am busy, and you really don't care how I am doing, so just get to the point."

So quickly identify the value you, your products or services may provide, ask for the appointment to discuss it further and get off the phone. For example:

> "Mr. Johnson, my organization has been instrumental in helping many companies in the Bay Area reduce their long distance bill by as much as 50%, while at the same time enhancing communication with their staff. My name is Todd Johnson, and I represent XYZ Telecommunications. The purpose of my call is to ask you a few questions to determine if you can receive these benefits also."

Remember, that prospect probably already has enough friends, but never enough profit.

## Chain Yourself to the Desk

The key to telephone prospecting success lies in developing your rhythm. You need to force yourself to remain at your desk until you make your 30 minutes of phone calls. The only reason you should not be on the phone during that period is that you are writing or typing what just transpired on the last call. Many salespeople will make one call, and then get a cup of coffee; make another call, and then go to the restroom, make another call, and then...By the time they do all of that, time is up. Successful sales professionals form the habit of doing things unsuccessful sales professionals don't do.

## Speak with Enthusiasm and Confidence

While developing one of my courses, I interviewed several top level executives and their executive assistants. Without fail, they all identified how important it is that the sales professional calling exhibit both enthusiasm and confidence. For the executive assistant the appearance of confidence is important because they have to quickly determine if they should allow the salesperson to speak to the top level contact (TLC) they support. They said that if you came across as being unsure of yourself or lacking confidence, their decision is rather simple. They will not allow you to get through to the TLC.

Confidence is a remarkable trait. Most people for some reason are attracted to others who are confident—not arrogant, but confident. At the same time, most people tend to reject those who seem to lack confidence. Just look at your own day-to-day dealings. Do you prefer a surgeon, mechanic, barber, coach, teacher, or repair person (the list could go on forever) who has confidence in their abilities or one without? I am sure we agree that we would much rather work with the individual that displays reasonable self-assurance.

It is also important to speak in a conversational tone. Talk as though you are speaking to a friend, neighbor, or family member; someone that you are comfortable with and enjoy speaking with. You should also practice voice inflection when using the telephone. Remember, your voice is the only tool you have while on the telephone. You must make the most of it.

Be careful to raise and lower your inflection on key words or points in your conversation. It is a good idea to record your voice on your own voice mail or recording device, and listen to it in order to determine if your voice sounds friendly and natural. It would also be a good idea to let others close to you listen to your recording and provide feedback as to whether or not you sound natural, conversational, and confident.

## Handling Objections on the Telephone

Even if you give the best 30-Second Commercial in the history of mankind, you will still run into resistance from your prospects or customers. Every phone call is a distraction. The person you are contacting is more than likely doing something else when you called. Therefore, it is natural for him or her to provide what I call "reflex resistance." When attempting to sell your products or services, the objections you receive are reflex resistances. Most people have three to four sure-fire objections that normally get rid of the average sales professional. Admit it. You even use them when you receive calls at home. You may use some of the following if you are the customer or hear them if you are the salesperson:

"I'm not interested."
"We just bought one."
"I'm busy right now."
"Please put me on your do-not-call list."

If you are calling a business, you may hear the following:
"We are not interested."
"I don't want to waste your time or mine."
"See me after the first of the year (or slow season)."

"We only do business with XYZ Company."
"See my manager or purchasing agent."
"Too busy."
"I don't see salespeople."
"Just send me some literature."

I am going to provide you with some proven responses to handle these seemingly difficult objections.

## Standard Responses to Objections

### *"We are not interested."*

I realize that at this time you are not interested, Mr. Prospect. My purpose for contacting you is to schedule a brief appointment to learn more about your direction for your company and then determine how I may assist you. Is there an opportunity for us to meet this week or should we consider next week?

### *"I don't want to waste your time or mine."*

With all due respect, anytime I get to explore the possible benefits and value that we can provide to companies like yours is certainly not a waste of my time, and I sincerely do not feel it will be a waste of your time. Mr./Mrs. Prospect, if I am in your office longer than fifteen minutes it will be because you have asked me to stay. May we go ahead and schedule a brief appointment now?

### *"See me after the first of the year (or slow season)."*

That's exactly why I would like to see you now. I'm sure you'll agree that the best time to consider new ideas that could be helpful is at a time when you can carefully consider the advantages rather than a time when you must hastily make a decision. My purpose for contacting you now is to gain an understanding of your goals and provide some new ideas for your consideration at the appropriate time.

### "We only do business with XYZ Company."

You remind me of many of my clients. We have quite a few clients that use both XYZ and us, and my clients like that arrangement because they feel they get the best of both worlds. Suppose for a moment that there were some ideas exclusive to us that are of value to your organization, wouldn't you at least want to be aware of them? Can we invest fifteen minutes together to determine if we can be of assistance to you in reaching your objectives?

### "See my manager or purchasing agent."

Mr./Mrs. Prospect, I realize that you are ultimately responsible for the overall operation and profitability of the company. Therefore, I wanted to meet with you briefly and find out the direction you want to take your organization. Then I would be better prepared to meet with whomever you recommend and provide long-term solutions instead of short-term gains. May we meet next week for fifteen minutes or would the following week fit into your schedule?

### "Too busy."

Mr. Prospect, busy executives like yourself are my best clients. In fifteen minutes, I can ask you a few questions to identify your company goals and any issues that may hinder you from reaching your objectives. Then, we would be able to present some ideas that may have merit for your organization. Mr. Prospect, if I am there longer than fifteen minutes, it will be because you asked me to stay. Why don't we look at our schedules now for the most convenient time to meet?

### *"I don't see salespeople."*

I apologize if I gave you the impression that I was contacting someone in your position to sell something. My purpose for contacting you is to schedule a brief appointment to find out your long-range objectives and briefly discuss how we have helped other companies (either in the area or in their industry). If you feel there are advantages to our ideas after our fifteen minute appointment, I will be pleased to speak with whom you deem appropriate.

### *"Just send me some literature."*

That's exactly why I wanted you to invest fifteen minutes with me. We have a tremendous amount of research information on topics that affect or enhance organizational performance. Once we meet and you share your vision and direction for your company, I will be better able to provide pertinent information on issues your company my be facing now or could experience in the future. (Then ask for the appointment.)

Although these objections may seem insurmountable, they really are not. The sales professional who can respond to three or four of these objections in a conversational tone usually gets an appointment. It is amazing how many of us quit too soon.

The key to your success is in memorizing and rehearsing the responses until it sounds like you are having a conversation with someone. I repeat, your response should sound like you are having a conversation, with the appropriate conversational tone and voice inflection. It should not sound like you are reading a script or as though you recently attended a training class and picked up some new tricks. Furthermore, it should not come across as though you are having a sparring match with words.

## Call Frequency

One of the most common questions I receive from participants in my training class is, "How often should I call?" or "When should I stop calling?" Your call frequency depends on the opportunity at hand. If you have uncovered an opportunity with a quick turnaround or short window of opportunity, you may need to call twice per week. If you are pursuing an organization to develop a relationship with hopes of future business, you may call once a month, or once every three months. It all depends on the potential for business.

The answer to, "When should I stop calling?" is simpler. Never! As a matter of fact, you should stop calling an account only if they say the following, "If you don't stop calling here, we will change the name of our company, all of our phone numbers, and send the authorities after you." The sad fact is that most sales professionals lack tenacity.

I read an article several years ago in which a survey was done with sales professionals. The survey reported the following:
- 42% of sales professionals quit after making one phone call attempt.
- 18% of sales professionals quit after making a second call.
- 25% of sales professionals quit after making a third call.
- Only 10 % continue to call indefinitely.
- It took five to eight calls to get the appointment and subsequent sale.

Think about it; 85% of the sales professionals surveyed quit after making just three calls. Imagine how much easier that makes it for the tenacious individuals to get business. Imagine how much money you leave on the table if you are one of the 85%.

I have interviewed a multitude of executives who confirmed the data from the survey. They said that on numerous occasions a salesperson will call and leave one or two voice mails. They will say something that stimulates reasonable interest on the part of the executive. The executive awaits the next call to learn more about their services or schedule the appointment…and the next call never comes.

In many instances, you may feel like a nuisance if you continue to pursue an executive. To the contrary, most successful people appreciate persistence. As a matter of fact, persistence is what got them where they are, and it is a trait that they admire and appreciate when they see it in others.

I recently began conducting training with a commercial real estate company, and I reiterated that most prospects appreciate courteous determination. A few weeks after the class, one of the brokers commented that he closed a sizeable opportunity because he exhibited courteous determination. The client commented that the salesperson's persistence impressed him, and that he expected him to be that tenacious in finding tenants and buyers for the properties that he was assigning to the broker.

Another training company was developing a training program on how to penetrate large corporate accounts. They interviewed Fortune 500 CEOs, and asked the question, "How do we (sales professionals) get to you?" The response was:

1. First, you must be very persistent.
2. Secondly, if you get my attention, be prepared.
3. Lastly, when you get in front of me, don't pitch me product. Talk to me about where I want to take my company and what has to happen to get there.

Please note that the first thing the executives referenced as a condition for success is persistence.

## Handling Voice Mail

The issue of whether or not to leave a voice mail when attempting to contact a decision maker by telephone is another area that divides many sales professionals. Some believe that you should never leave a voice mail, but keep calling until the person answers their telephone. There are some who believe you should leave a voice mail only after you have attempted to reach them several times. There are others who believe you should leave a voice mail each time that you are unable to make contact. I am inclined to agree with the "leave a voice mail each time" group.

Remember, most successful people appreciate persistence. How do they know that you are being persistent if you don't leave the messages?

## What Message Should I Leave?

Basically, the message you can leave is an enhanced 30-Second Commercial. Let's revisit my commercial from when I was in the furniture industry, and convert it to a voice mail message.

*"Mr. Johnson, my organization has been instrumental in helping many of our clients get improved performance from their three greatest resources: their real estate, their people, and their technology."*

*"As a matter of fact, we recently provided one of our clients with an idea that helped them get 25% more people into their current facility which alleviated the need to lease additional space. That greatly improved their profit picture."*

*"My name is Tye Maner and I represent Herman Miller. The purpose of my call is to schedule a brief appointment with you to*

*learn more about your vision or direction for your company to determine how or if we can help you reach your objectives."*

*"I regret that I missed you, and I will call again next week. In the event you would like to reach me sooner, my telephone number is xxx-xxx-xxxx. Again, my name is Tye Maner, and my number is xxx-xxx-xxxx. I look forward to speaking with you soon. Have a great day!"*

CHAPTER TEN

# Buying Signals

An age old question is, "When do you ask for the order?" The answer is simple; when the customer is ready to buy. Buying signals are powerful signs indicating your prospect or client's potential willingness to move forward with the sale. The majority of the population cannot control buying signals. I have taken several negotiation courses, and have even developed my own course on negotiations. And with all of this training, I still slip and provide buying signals when someone does a great job of linking their products or services to my needs. Buying signals can occur very quickly. You must train yourself to recognize them. There are two types of buying signals: verbal and physical. As a rule, true buying signals normally occur after you have presented your product(s) or service(s) and the prospect or customer clearly understands the value it can provide to them.

Too often, sales professionals totally miss multiple buying signals from p/c's. The p/c shows great interest and the salesperson allows them to leave without attempting to close the opportunity. The inability to recognize buying signals can prolong the sales cycle unnecessarily, or even cause the sale to be lost, because the p/c's interest wanes or the next salesperson doesn't miss the opportunity.

A few years ago, I worked with a company in the Midwest. My assignment was to go out on appointments with their salespersons and give them feedback after each sales call. There was a particular call we made where the prospects were asking many questions that I recognized as buying signals.

The salesperson I was working with answered all of their questions, however, did not recognize the questions as opportunities to potentially close the sale that day. We concluded the meeting, and headed for the door. I did not feel it was appropriate for me to say anything because I was not an agent of the company. Yet, it was virtually impossible for me to not attempt to close an opportunity staring me in the face. I wrestled with myself silently as we were about to leave the office; "Should I intervene or just provide feedback after the call?" Ultimately the sales professional in me won out over the coach in me. I turned around as we got to the door, and said, "Based on what Sarah shared with you today, do you feel comfortable that her solution can provide the results you are looking to achieve?"

The two decision-makers we were meeting with turned and looked at each other and paused for about five seconds. They both nodded their heads as one of them said "Yes." I said, "Well, can we go ahead and place the order today so you can start enjoying the benefits she described?" They looked at each other again with another pause, nodded and one of them said, "Sure."

The salesperson's chin almost hit the floor. She could not believe that she had been so close to a sale and was about to walk away from it. She later wondered aloud how many other opportunities she had allowed to slip through her fingers, how many thousands of dollars in commissions she lost over the years by waiting for prospect to say, "We'll take it," or "Write it up," instead of being proactive instead of patient.

The following are some examples of buying signals.

**Verbal Buying Signals**

Verbal Buying Signals are provided in statements or questions. Some examples of statement buying signals are:

> This is exactly what we are looking for.
> I think John will be pleased with this.

Some examples of question buying signals are:

> How much is it?
> Is it difficult to use?
> What colors do you offer?
> How soon can you deliver it?
> How soon can I move in?
> What is the warranty?
> Who else has it in my business?
> What forms of payment do you accept?
> How many do you have in stock?

It does not necessarily indicate a willingness to purchase when you hear only one question buying signal. However, when you get two or three question buying signals one after another, you should take their temperature to see if they are ready to close. That is called "testing the water," which we will talk about in the next chapter.

**Physical Buying Signals**

Physical Buying Signals also occur quickly and are easy to miss. Be alert. Some examples of physical buying signals are as follows:

## The Customer Becomes Friendly

This doesn't mean a prospect asks you out for a date. You will notice that the prospect will become more cordial or open, whereas, he or she was once aloof or less willing to divulge information to you. This is a very good sign.

## The Sparkling Eyes

You will notice that when you say or do something that appeals to the prospect, his eyes will sparkle and/or his eyebrows will rise. Another sign is they may turn and look at an associate. For example, suppose I was presenting to two decision-makers, and I said, "Our system will allow you to reduce your cost by a nickel per transaction." Both of their eyebrows raise and they look at each other without saying a word. But, what they are saying with their reaction could be, "Did you hear what he just said? We do 2,000,000 transactions per week. That would be a huge cost reduction."

## Reexamination of Your Product or Service

Often, when someone is genuinely interested in the product or service you provide, they will want to reexamine it before they make their final decision. In a recent survey I took with participants of my workshops, they stated that 80 - 95% of the time the p/c's made the purchase if they inquired a second time. Think about it from your perspective How many times have you taken a second look at the following?
- Home/Apartment
- Car
- Television/stereo
- School
- Furniture
- Clothing

You probably agree that you make purchases in the same manner. Unfortunately, in far too many instances this is a missed opportunity for many sales professionals to close the sale. "Thanks again for stopping by or calling us, and let us know if you have any more questions," is the customary response from those who miss this buying signal.

## Hand on Chin

Believe it or not, this is one of the greatest buying signals around. They are imagining themselves utilizing your product or service and have taken mental ownership.

The first time I remember seeing this signal was in a presentation I provided to a prospect. We were only five minutes into my presentation. I had just concluded giving my third feature and benefit, and the prospect placed his hand on his chin. He then turned away from me and began to look around the room. After a brief period of silence, he said, "I wonder where I can put it?" (referring to the product I was presenting). He had taken ownership and the presentation was over. At this point, many sales professionals continue to try to sell. This is known as talking past the sale.

## Testing the Water

Everyone who reads this book takes a shower or a bath on a regular basis. You turn the water on. You place your hand or foot in the water to make sure it is safe or comfortable to get into.

If the water is too hot or too cold, you make the proper adjustment, and test again. When the temperature feels right, you get in. That is exactly what we are doing with the p/c once you recognize buying signals. Testing the water prevents you from closing prematurely and causing an uncomfortable or awkward situation for you and the prospect. It also eliminates you from missing opportunities to close the sale.

A closing question asks for a decision. It could be premature. Testing the water includes asking for an opinion. Once you receive several favorable responses to your testing, then you ask for the order.

Suppose that your prospect asks a couple of questions (which are buying signals) after you have illustrated how your product or service can clearly satisfy one or more of their needs. The third question they ask is, "How much is it?" You realize that these questions are possible indications of their willingness to move forward with the sale. Therefore, you:

    1) Acknowledge their question - "I can appreciate that it is important to make sure your choice falls within your acceptable price range."

    2) Test the water - "If we can provide you with a "_____" that satisfies both your requirements and falls within your acceptable price, would you be willing to move forward?"

If the prospect's response is "Yes," then go ahead and discuss how much it costs and options for them to pay for it. You may have to negotiate at this point, or find an alternative product that meets their needs, but falls under a lower price point.

If the prospect's response is "No," don't panic. This just tells you that there is more selling to do. You would then say, "It appears that you may still have some questions that we haven't answered yet. Do you mind if I ask what they are?" Do not ask if they have any concerns; ask if they have any questions. Questions are easier to address.

The client will probably raise another question. At that point, you should probe to make sure that you are clear regarding this new need or want.

The customer now gives an additional concern.

| Customer: | "We also need to know about how soon you can deliver it." |
| --- | --- |
| Salesperson: | "It sounds like the delivery is an important consideration for you. Tell me more about that." |
| Customer: | "We need to have the new system operational by the first week of November." |
| Salesperson: | "I understand; and why is that deadline so important for your company?" |
| Customer: | "We are on a tight deadline to complete a project for one our biggest clients, and if the system is up and running by the first week of November, we will have plenty of time to successfully complete the project and meet our commitment to the client." |
| Salesperson: | "What do you think would be the consequences if your new system was not operational by the first week of November?" |
| Customer: | "We may miss our completion date which would place our client in a very difficult position. We may have to compensate the client for our failure, and may even lose the client." |

| Salesperson: | "I fully understand the importance of your timeline. Are there any other questions we need to address for you?" |
|---|---|
| Customer: | "No." |
| Salesperson: | So, if we can provide you with a system that falls within your acceptable price range, and you felt comfortable that it could be operational by the first week of November to meet your tight deadline for one of your biggest clients, would you be willing to move forward?" |
| Customer: | "Yes, I would." |

Now all you have to do is work through the areas of price and delivery with the client and you have earned their business.

Keep in mind that we want to expose all of the client's concerns before we start addressing them one at a time.

First, it is important to always acknowledge the prospects question before testing the water. Otherwise, it may appear as though you are only interested in closing the sale. Acknowledging is a response reflecting your acceptance of their feelings. Below are some examples.

"I can appreciate that you would want to..."

"I can see how that would be important to you."

"I understand that the delivery date is critical for you."

Secondly, it is also important to test the water in a conversational tone, as if you are just chatting with a close friend. Too often, a salesperson will turn from Dr. Jekyll to Mr. Hyde when they are approaching the close. The salesperson goes from friendly to overly aggressive or from friendly to very serious. In most cases this disturbs the prospect and makes him or her feel uneasy.

Below are some examples of testing the water.

- "If we were able to show you how everyone can operate this system with a few moments of instruction, would this be the system for you?"

- "Just suppose for a moment that we could find a location that is available for that date, would you like to secure that site?"

- "Based on what you have seen today, do you feel comfortable that our services can provide the results you are looking to achieve?"

If you receive a favorable response, then it is time to ask for the order.

CHAPTER ELEVEN

# Asking For the Order

Once you have tested the water and received a favorable response, the next step is to ask for the order.

There was a period early in my sales career when there were a multitude of books published on closing the sale. They had dozens of techniques to help you close the sale such as the following titles:

The Inflation close

The Ben Franklin close

The Lost Sale close

The Call Back close

The Think It Over close

The Order Blank close

The list of closes could go on for pages. Some of the closing techniques were over a page long and you had to memorize them word for word. Many of the closes are outdated and make the salesperson appear to be a con-man, only out for the sale, and not concerned about the needs of the customer. Today, customers are far more informed and would be insulted by many of the techniques used decades ago. Your customer does not mind buying. They don't want to feel like they were sold.

However, there are some ways to ask for the order that are simple, legitimate ways to bring closure to the sale.

## Ways to Ask For the Order

### Ask

The best way to ask for the order is to just ask. "You do not have because you do not ask." Although that statement is from a scripture in the Bible, it is true as to why salespersons miss sales opportunities. You are afraid to ask because the answer may be "No." That should no longer be a concern because you now understand that you ask for the order when the client is ready to purchase by testing the water first. Stop waiting for the customer to say, "I'll take it," or "Let's do it." You could prolong the sale by days, weeks, or even months waiting for the client to initiate the order.

Below are some ways to ask for the order:
1. Is there any reason why we can't do business today?
2. What would have to happen for us to do business today?
3. Can we go ahead and place the order now?
4. When would you like delivery of your _____?
5. When would you like installation?
6. If I were to ask you to do business today, what would your answer be?
7. Would you prefer lease or purchase outright?
8. What do we need to do to get a purchase order?
9. Do you see any reason why you shouldn't start enjoying these benefits today?
10. What is our next step; can we write it up today?
11. Where do we stand in the decision-making process?

## Order Blank Close

This is the most fundamental of all closing devices. You begin by asking your customer a question. Fill out the answer on your order blank, contract or agreement. For example, what is your name? What is your correct mailing address? As long as the customer does not stop you, they have bought. Continue asking questions until you have completed the form. When you get to the bottom of the form, swing it around and hand the customer your pen and ask him or her to okay it for you.

## Alternate Choice

> "Mr./Ms. Prospect, which do you feel will meet your needs best...the "_____" or the "_____?"
> "Do you normally use cash to acquire your new products or would you prefer our easy investment plan?"

## 1 – 10 Close

Simply ask the client, "On a scale of one to ten, one being that you see very little use or benefit from what we are offering and ten being that you see benefits and merit and you want to acquire it, where do we stand?" The next question to ask is, "What do we need to do to get to a ten."

CHAPTER TWELVE

# Referrals – The Pot of Gold at the End of the Sale

How many times have you been in the market for a product or service, and asked a friend, family member, or associate for their recommendation? At some time or another, we have all sought a reference on some or all of the items listed below:

- A mechanic
- A dentist
- A realtor
- A restaurant
- A school
- A class
- A repairman
- A barber or beautician
- A vehicle
- A vacation spot
- A hotel
- Electronics
- Software
- Computer
- An instructor
- A cell phone or cell phone service provider
- A movie

The list could go on for days. The bottom line is we have greater confidence in purchasing a product or using a service when someone we know and respect had a favorable experience and highly recommends it. In many instances, once we receive a recommendation by someone we trust, we look no further or place their choice at the top of our list.

Recently, a young man was going door-to-door in my neighborhood selling a cleaning product. I talked to him briefly, but had no interest in the product. I found out later that he went to another home in the neighborhood and mentioned to them that I liked the product and purchased it. Obviously, he lied to them. However, believing that I had purchased the product made my neighbors more comfortable with buying it.

The referral is an easier and more effective way to find new opportunities than the cold call. The referral is also the best way to close business quickly. To get a referral you simply ask someone you know or have done business with to provide the names of their friends, family, associates, or colleagues that may be able to use your products or services.

The referral is the reward you receive for a job well done. Your closing rate becomes extremely high on these opportunities. My business was built on this approach. As a matter of fact, ninety-seven percent of my business is based on referrals. Most of the successful sales professionals I know have used this simple technique to add to their client list. By using this approach they worked smarter, not harder.

Surprisingly, most salespersons don't ask for referrals on a regular basis.

I'll never forget the time I was conducting a seminar and had just finished talking about the importance of asking for referrals and how easy it is to find new opportunities by doing so. One of the participants raised his hand, and he wanted to affirm my statement. He then said, "You are right about that, because I asked for a referral once and it worked." He went on to say that he ultimately won a sale from that referral. It was amazing to me that it worked yet he only used it that one time. How many times do we try something that works, then we file it away or put it on a shelf and never use it again? Asking for referrals makes more sense than any other form of prospecting. The person to whom you are referred is more receptive to you because someone they trust or respect had enough faith and confidence to recommend you.

The following is an approach to getting a referral that I found to be very successful. After completing a project with my client, I would pay a follow up visit to confirm that they were satisfied with the outcome of our work.  The dialogue would normally go as follows:

Me:     "Tom, I requested this meeting to confirm that we met and hopefully exceeded your expectations for this project."

Client:   "Tye, we are really pleased with the results you and your company provided."

Me:     "I am pleased to hear that, Tom. I am just curious, what benefits do you feel your organization derived from our business relationship?"

Client:   "Well, the morale of the staff seems to have improved, as well as their efficiency."

Me:     "And what do you feel the improved morale and efficiency will mean to your company?"

Client:    "It could mean several things. If all employees are happy, our turnover numbers will be greatly reduced which will also lower our training and recruitment costs. Those two things alone will positively impact our operating cost. If our employees are more efficient, that will assure that we meet our project deadlines, which will assist us in hitting our revenue numbers."

Me:    "I am glad to hear that we were able to have such a positive impact on your organization, and to assist you in reaching your objectives. There are many companies who are currently facing these or other issues that we may be able to assist also. You may even know some other organizations that we can help. Who else do you know that we may be able to assist?"

Client:    "Now that you mention it, I do know someone that may be able to use your services. His name is Adam Smith."

Me:    "What company does Mr. Smith work for and what is his title, and phone number?"

Client:    "He is the President of ABC Company and his telephone number is 555-1212."

Me:    "Thank you, for directing me to Mr. Smith. I will contact him next week. I really hope that I am not pressing my luck, but would it be possible for you to place a call now to Mr. Smith and let him know that I will be calling him? "

Client:    "That won't be a problem at all."

Let's dissect what occurred in my dialogue with the customer. The first thing I wanted to do was get him to say that our relationship was beneficial to him and his company. (One of the greatest rules of selling is to never tell someone what you can ask them. If you tell them they doubt it, if they say it, it is true.) There is always the possibility that the client may have been displeased with our performance. If this is the case, we would still need to know that they were unhappy so we can solve the issues and please the client. Once they are delighted with our performance, then we can proceed with asking for the referral. We can still get referrals from a customer even when we dropped the ball in service, as long as we resolve the concern of the customer promptly.

After Tom stated the value he felt his company received from my company and my services, I wanted him to explore what this value really meant to his organization. He reminded himself of the positive impact we will have on his organization's profitability and performance. We talked about how other companies are faced with the same decisions and are trying to find proper solutions. Tom now has an opportunity to assist his friends and colleagues in solving issues relative to their companies.

"Who else do you know that we may be able to assist," was the next question that I asked. This question will get you more referrals than any other question you could ask. It is an open-ended question that elicits a thought-out response. Many salespersons use closed-ended questions that are easy to say "No" to. Some examples are:

"Do you know anyone else that can use our services?"
Or even worse,

"You don't know anyone else that we can help, do you?"

Your call to Adam Smith will not be a cold call. It is now a warm call because someone that Adam knows and trusts has had a favorable experience with you, and in many cases Mr. Johnson's endorsement is sufficient for him.

In the event Mr. Smith is located in the same building, your first goal is to get a physical introduction to him by Mr. Johnson. This provides instant credibility. The next best approach is for Mr. Johnson to call on my behalf. The final option is for the client to send an e-mail. The first two choices work best because the prospect can sense the enthusiasm and passion of the client either in person or on the phone.

We just explored how to get a referral from a new client that you have completed work for. So, when is it a good idea to ask for a referral from at an existing client? The answer is simple: always.

Although the strongest referrals come from someone who has already had a positive experience with your product or services, there are also other occasions to ask for a referral.

You may ask for a referral prior to closing the sale or immediately after you have closed the sale. You may ask, "Mr. Johnson, who do you know that owns their own business (or lives next door, or who was just promoted, or has moved into the area, or what ever kind of prospect you're particularly looking for)?" Help the person focus on a specific area in his or her group of known contacts. Make it easy for the person to help you. Repeat the process until you get several names.

How do you know which types of prospects to ask for? That depends on where you think your best customers will come from in the near future? If you want to focus on contractors, you could ask, "Mr. Smith, who do you know in the contracting business?"

Qualify the referrals. Suppose the person has given you three names. Let him or her qualify them. Ask, "If you were me, which of these people would you contact first?" After they prioritize the list, find out the reason for the first choice. "That's interesting. Why did you select Mary Jones first?" Now Mr. Johnson may give you key information that you can use in selling to the referred prospect.

In some cases, the client will give you the names of other potential prospects but may not feel comfortable giving a personal endorsement. That is fine. In this scenario, get the client to become your coach on the prospect. A coach is someone who wants you to succeed and is willing to help you with no vested interest. Find out the following information:

- What is the best day/time to contact prospect?
- What are some of prospects hobbies?
- What are the prospects likes and dislikes?
- What topics should you avoid?
- What may be some primary concerns for the prospect?
- What is the prospect passionate about?
- Is it acceptable to say that Mr. Johnson's organization has used your company's services?

By asking these questions, you will gain valuable insight into the prospect and the ways to contact and win them over, although you were not able to get a personal endorsement from the client.

Ask for referrals with the same frequency that you brush your teeth - several times a day.

## Referral Letters

The referral letters is another valuable tool. It is a must have in every salesperson's tool box. I cannot count the number of sales that I have won over the years because of these testimonials. I had a three-ring binder full of them that could satisfy any customer concern. The following are some of the categories in which I grouped the letters :

- Service performance
- Product performance
- Company performance
- My individual performance

I showed my prospects other companies and decision-makers who may have had similar concerns to their's and were pleased with the results they received from working with my organization. In most instances, this made them feel more comfortable in moving forward with a decision to do business with us. This is how the conversation normally went when I used the testimonial letters to close the opportunity.

> Me:     "Well, Mr. Smith, based on our presentation and discussion do you feel comfortable that we can provide the results that you are looking to achieve?"

> Mr. Smith:     "Well, I think so (sounding uncertain about something)."

> Me:     "It sounds like you have a question that we have not addressed. Do you mind if I asked what your question is?"

Mr. Smith: "It's not that we don't think your product will do the job. We have had problems with service after the sale with another vendor and we want to make sure we don't have that experience again."

Me: "I appreciate your candor, and thank you for sharing that with me. Just to clarify, specifically what type of problems did you have with service?"

Mr. Smith: "We never saw the salesperson again after the sale was made and the product was installed. On most occasions, it would take them at least a week to respond to our service calls."

Me: "I can see why you would be concerned about receiving that type of service again. What was the impact on your company when you received such slow response?"

Mr. Smith: "It put us behind in production. In some instances, we even missed a few important deadlines. On two occasions, we had to outsource work that we could've done if the product was working correctly or serviced promptly."

Me: "Thank you Mr. Smith. That clarifies things for me. In addition to this, are there any questions you would like for me to address?"

Mr. Smith: "No, this is our primary concern."

Me:     "So, if you felt that not only were we providing you with a very reliable product, but we would also take care of any service concerns in a prompt and responsive manner, would you be willing to move forward with an agreement today?"

Mr. Smith: "I don't see any reason why we couldn't do business if I had the comfort level you just described."

Me:     "You're not alone, Mr. Smith. We have had many clients raise similar questions. I would like to share with you some of the comments we have received from our clients after using our products and experiencing our level of service and commitment."

It appears that Mr. Smith has two concerns that are hindering us from moving forward with the sale; he was concerned about the product performance, and our ability to respond promptly when the product needed service.

At this point, I would get my three-ring binder which held dozens of testimonials. Together we would look at several letters under the product performance category. Mr. Smith normally recognized the names of many of the companies we had done business with and in some cases the name of the individual who wrote the letter. Next, we would view a few letters under the service performance category. Again, he may recognize company and individual names that have had a positive experience. The letters had key points highlighted with a marker. This eliminated having to read the entire letter in order to get the essence of it.

Whenever possible, I would have the prospect read the highlighted portions.

After reviewing several letters, I would say:

Me:    "Would you agree that normally you have to feel strongly about something, either positively or negatively to take the time to write a letter?"

Mr. Smith:    "That's a fair statement."

Me:    "The letters we just reviewed were written by businessmen like you. Do these letters address how we and our products perform after the sale?"

Mr. Smith:    "Yes."

Me:    "Can we go ahead and place the order today so you and (insert company name here) can begin enjoying the benefits we've discussed?"

Mr. Smith:    "Let's get started."

As I mentioned, the referral letter approach has won me and other sales professionals countless opportunities. Most people feel comfortable moving forward when they know that others have made the same decision and are pleased with the results. There is no technique that works 100% of the time. However, you will see a dramatic improvement in your closing rate when you apply this proven technique.

# Conclusion

I have been in the sales and marketing arenas for over twenty years and have trained over 10,000 salespersons. As a salesperson, I have tasted both bitter failure and tremendous success. Fortunately, the successes have far outweighed the failures. As strange as this may seem, I learned the most from the failures. At times the failures were so painful. I did my best to ensure that I would not have to experience them again. From the failures came a burning desire to hone my skills so that I would not allow history to repeat itself. I would be prepared for the opportunities. I am truly thankful for the pains in my life and my career. If it were not for those occurrences, you would not be reading this book.

My purpose in writing this book is to provide you with insight that will assist you in attaining your goals and aspirations. This book can help you make a tremendous living, provide for your family, assist in the growth of your company, and contribute to your community. Someone once made the statement, "Nothing happens until something is sold." Think about what would happen to the economy and world if nothing was sold for an entire day, week or, heaven forbid, a month. The world would come to a complete stop.

Truly, sales is a wonderful vocation. Like all professions, there is a certain element that gives the entire profession a bad name. There are those who lie, cheat and steal from customers for their own gain. They don't last long in our profession; however, their actions and treachery leaves a long bad taste with the customers they abused and took advantage of.

My primary goal in writing this book is to educate, motivate, and in some instances, rejuvenate you. I always felt that if I got one good idea from a book I read, the book would be worth the investment of time to read it. As I stated in my introduction, it is my desire and belief that you will walk away with innovative ideas, tremendous techniques, and sustainable skills that will elevate you to the next level in your quest as a student of your profession.